TRUE BEER

INSIDE THE SMALL, NEIGHBORHOOD
NANOBREWERIES CHANGING
THE WORLD OF CRAFT BEER

Timothy Sprinkle

Skyhorse Publishing

Skyhorse Publishing books may be purchased in bulk at special discounts for sales promotion, corporate gifts, fund-raising, or educational purposes. Special editions can also be created to specifications. For details, contact the Special Sales Department, Skyhorse Publishing, 307 West 36th Street, 11th Floor, New York, NY 10018 or info@skyhorsepublishing.com.

Skyhorse® and Skyhorse Publishing® are registered trademarks of Skyhorse Publishing, Inc.®, a Delaware corporation.

Visit our website at www.skyhorsepublishing.com.

10 9 8 7 6 5 4 3 2 1

Library of Congress Cataloging-in-Publication Data

Names: Sprinkle, Timothy, author.
Title: True beer : inside the small, neighborhood nanobreweries
    changing the world of craft beer / Timothy Sprinkle.
Description: New York, NY : Skyhorse Publishing, [2016] | Includes
    bibliographical references.
Identifiers: LCCN 2016020597| ISBN 9781634506427 (pbk. : alk. paper) | ISBN
    9781634506434 (Ebook)
Subjects: LCSH: Microbreweries—United States. | Small business—United
    States. | Beer—United States. | Brewing—United States--Amateurs' manuals
Classification: LCC TP577 .S67 2016 | DDC 663/.420973--dc23 LC record available at
    https://lccn.loc.gov/2016020597

Cover design by Laura Klynstra
Cover photo: iStockphoto

Printed in the United States of America

To all my drinking buddies,
past, present, and future.

CONTENTS

INTRODUCTION

*T*hink the beer business is all fun and games? Think again. During the 2015 Super Bowl broadcast, Anheuser-Busch InBev ran an ad that came across as nothing short of a shot across the bow of the craft brewing industry and its customers.

"Budweiser, proudly a macro beer," the spot announces. "It's not brewed to be fussed over; it's brewed for a crisp smooth finish. This is the only beer beechwood aged since 1876. There's only one Budweiser. It's brewed for drinking, not dissecting. The people who drink our beer are people who like to drink beer. Brewed the hard way. Let them sip their pumpkin peach ale, we'll be brewing some golden suds. This is the famous Budweiser beer. This Bud's for you."

Those were strong words in beer circles, and they upset many people in the craft side of the industry, including Larry Bell of Bell's Brewery in Kalamazoo, Michigan, a craft brewer that produces about 250,000 barrels per year and has been around since 1983. He told the *Detroit News* that he just about jumped out of his chair when he saw the Super Bowl ad. So what was his response? The next day, Bell got to work on a limited edition run of his own Bell's Pumpkin Peach Ale that he personally brewed on his pilot system and sold out of the Bell's taproom shortly thereafter, the proceeds of which he donated to a local nonprofit.

"We're starting to eat their lunch," Bell told the newspaper regarding the rise of craft beer in the industry as a whole. "Budweiser sales have basically been plummeting . . . but typically in the industry you don't go after somebody else's beer, you promote your own."

Sam Calagione, the founder of Dogfish Head Brewing Company, agreed, describing the incident with the ad as a great thing for craft beer in general.

"It shows how confused and conflicted the world's biggest brewery is about how to engage an American populous whose beer tastes are changing," he told *Men's Journal* at the time. "The more they spite us for trying beer outside of the light lager juggernaut, the more we're going to stand for something very separate from what they're about. Then as they buy out the companies making the beers they're making fun of, the hypocrisy is very apparent. I'm sure there's a room full of MBAs and all they care about is the Budweiser brand. That's what they're paid to care about. They don't give a shit if promoting Bud means making fun of other brands in the A-B InBev network. It shows that true craft brewers are brewers first, businesspeople second. That company is run by nothing but businesspeople."

The ad even provoked strong reactions among the other macrobrewers. Miller-Coors, for example, released a statement shortly after the spot aired, extolling its belief that all beers should be fussed over. "Quality isn't something that belongs to a single style of beer or a single brewer," the company wrote. "It belongs to all of the people who deliver on the promise of consistently brewing and distributing the highest-quality, best-tasting beers in the world."

Before the Super Bowl itself was even over, Budweiser was backpedaling: "We're not anti-craft. Just pro-Bud," the company posted on its Twitter feed during the game.

The simple fact that consumer reactions to a multimillion-dollar Super Bowl advertisement created by a multinational beverage conglomerate generated this sort of ripple effect reaction in such a well-established, profitable industry is telling. In another example, craft beer blog *Hopstories* issued a video response on YouTube declaring: "We will savor our hundreds of styles, you keep pushing your one." Such reactions show that the macros' once insurmountable competitive advantage is shrinking. It shows that the products they have been producing for decades, largely unchanged, are no longer as popular or selling as well as they once were. And it shows that, as the beer-drinking public's tastes have changed and evolved, the traditional producers have not kept pace.

What's more, the rise of craft beer is hitting the macrobrewers where it matters most: in their profit and loss statements. More proof of this can be found in the increased consolidation that's swept through the industry in recent years. As of 2015, according to a report from Bank of America Merrill Lynch, just four companies—Anheuser-Busch InBev, SABMiller, Heineken, and Carlsberg—together brew about half the world's beer under a long list of different brand names. That's down from ten companies controlling just over 50 percent of the global market in 2004. Simply put, a strong and competitive market does not go through rapid consolidation like this. As much as anything, this is a sign of weakness across the board, of a circle-the-wagons mentality on the part of industry.

In short: craft brewing has been around for decades, but its time in the sun as a major part of the global beer industry is just beginning. This book is an attempt to capture this moment in time and chronicle this emerging trend in American life and business through the stories of the people involved and the work they do every day, particularly in the growing nano segment of the market.

The craft beer industry is full of upstart, independent breweries like those profiled in this book. They're small, they're agile, they brew tons of great beer, and, as startup businesses, they come with many of the same rewards (and challenges) that entrepreneurs in technology and other fields know well. The promise? Probably not riches, as food and beverage is a notoriously finicky field in that regard, but the creative factor is through the roof. Brewers get the chance to work with beer every day, to experiment with new recipes, and to develop their own manufacturing systems, all while making something tangible with their hands that makes people happy. In today's digital economy, this opportunity is tough for many would-be nanobrewers to turn down.

This is a book about beer. This is a book about business. But, most of all, this is a book about people—people who are working difficult manual labor jobs in a very competitive industry and against increasingly difficult odds. Colorado, for instance, is on pace to surpass three hundred craft breweries statewide by the end of the decade, all in an effort to produce something they believe in, that they're proud of, and that they want to share with the world.

The 3,400-plus craft brewers in the United States as of 2014 employ about 43,000 people, according to the Beer Institute, and generate more than $246 billion in overall economic impact. The staff at these breweries are doing this work—and let's be honest, this is real, backbreaking, physical labor—not because it's an easy path to great wealth but because they love the product, and they love being involved in an industry that's growing and evolving like craft beer is. Many of these people come from other backgrounds. Matthew Fuerst, the owner of Grandma's House, for example, is a technical writer by trade and had essentially no food-and-beverage training before embarking on his new venture. Regardless, these people still manage to make it work in this industry, getting up every morning and brewing beer simply because they can.

But craft beer, and nanobrewing in particular, is especially interesting in that way. It attracts all sorts: the engineers who want to get into the brewhouse and build their dream DIY system, the creative types who want to experiment with the flavors and styles, the entrepreneurs who want to build sustainable businesses, and the food-and-beverage experts who want to bring it all together as a fantastic experience for the customer. Brewing is so many things at once—a creative process, a manufacturing process, a business development process, a new type of restaurant and bar experience, and more.

With that in mind, I spent more than a year visiting with every small-time, neighborhood nanobrewer I could find, talking with them about everything from business development to real estate to the logistics of brewing at this scale. Then I went a step further and met with the suppliers: the farmers growing the ingredients, the middlemen selling them, the hardware experts building the brewhouses, and even the software developers bringing the age-old brewing process into the twenty-first century. Then I stepped back and looked at the industry and the community around it as a whole. The idea here is to offer a behind-the-scenes look at the nanobrewing segment of the craft brewing industry as it is right now, including all of the business forces that surround it and impact it every day.

This book primarily focuses on small, independent craft brewers in Colorado and nearby, in large part because the state is on the forefront of this brewing revolution. It is at the heart of one of the fastest-growing, most active beer markets in the country.

Colorado, after all, is the "Napa Valley of beer."

This book is a glimpse of what it's like to be a small, independent brewer in 2016, and it's harder than it looks.

CHAPTER 1

WHAT IS A NANOBREWERY?

*T*he landscape of American beer is changing. Again.

In the 1970s and '80s, the shift was from large corporate suppliers to smaller, independent "microbrewers," typified by producers such as The Boston Beer Company and Sierra Nevada Brewing Company, which focused their efforts on flavor and quality rather than sheer scale. They were able to find space in the market, because somewhere along the way America's taste for beer got lost in the watered-down lagers and "lite" beers that many of us have come to associate with the US industrial beer industry. We forgot what beer was supposed to taste like, what beer could taste like, and in the process, we lost a little bit of our shared food-and-beverage history. The early microbrewers woke up the country to that again.

But that was just the first step in an evolution still going on today.

Now the market is going even smaller, with tiny, independent brewers setting up shop in neighborhood brewhouses nationwide, focusing on crafting unique, flavorful brews specifically for their extremely local customer bases. They aren't selling thousands of barrels per week; they're thinking more in terms of dozens. They aren't bottling and distributing nationwide; they're only sending out the occasional keg to local restaurants and bars, preferring to sell directly out of their own taprooms. And they aren't building corporate empires; they're simply looking to serve their local customers, one pint at a time.

This is a new class of "nanobrewers" who are serving growing communities of drinkers looking for even more from their daily brew: something of higher quality, more unique, and that's more local both in terms of its ingredients as well as the people who make it. At the same time, these brewers are taking the microbrewers' focus on quality and flavor a step further, delving into unique new styles (like sours, imperials, and fresh hopped varieties) and experimenting with additions ranging from spices to teas, fruits, vegetables, and more. And they're doing it all at a scale, generally only a few barrels at a time, that lends itself to experimentation. Sure, that basil-grapefruit India Pale Ale might be amazing, but if it turns out not to be so amazing at least the brewer only has a few kegs to get rid of. By staying small, operators put only so much on the line. That's freeing for adventurous brewers, and it opens the door to experimentation and creativity that have never before been widely possible for many commercial brewers.

The model is unique. Most nanobrewing operations, or "nanos" as they're often known, sell their products directly to customers through their own on-site taprooms that often abut the production facilities themselves. If they do sell to outside vendors, it is generally only to a few local outlets at a time, as most brewers of this size simply don't have the production capacity to support greater distribution or rapid growth. They are small by design. That gives these taprooms—many of which do not even serve food—more of the feel of a neighborhood pub, a casual meeting spot for locals and craft beer lovers alike to gather, drink, and mingle.

This is the logical extension of a trend that's been growing in brewing circles since the 1970s, when a small group of British pub owners chose to produce their own small-batch cask ales in-house, rather than serving beers from the corporate producers of the time. This sell-what-you-brew approach took hold with a core group of small UK brewers—most notably Bill Urquhart, who had been the head brewer of the large Phipps Northampton Brewery before splitting off on his own to found the tiny Litchborough Brewery in 1974, specializing in the traditional beer styles of the British Isles—and eventually grew into a full-scale community of like-minded beer drinkers and producers.

But that was just the regional beginning of a movement that has now gone global. The reality is that, as of 2016, beer is in the midst of an ongoing renaissance in the United States, driven by a core group of dedicated craft brewers and tens of thousands of creative homebrewers, not to mention a beer-drinking public that has come to appreciate more complex and interesting flavors. The result: as of 2014, there were more than 3,400 breweries in the United States classified as craft operations—generally defined as small, independently owned commercial breweries that employ traditional brewing methods "with a focus on flavor and quality"—and they made up about 7.8 percent, or $14.3 billion, of the $100 billion-plus national beer market. The total number of all breweries jumped 19.4 percent between 2013 and 2014, and that's a staggering number, especially when you consider the local roots of craft beer and the still-limited distribution many brewers have access to. But it is indicative of the industry's exponential growth over the last thirty-odd years.

And you know what? That's still chump change in the face of the well-established, multibillion-dollar competition that is the industrial beer industry. These incumbents still dominate the market worldwide, producing far more product in far more places, and at cheaper prices, than craft brewers could ever hope to compete with. For example, global conglomerates like SABMiller and Anheuser-Busch InBev produce and sell more than 133 billion liters of beer per year on average, generating industry-wide revenues of nearly $300 billion. They're in just about every market in the world, own dozens of different brands, and remain the most widely available beers on the planet, as likely to show up in the jungles of Brazil as they are the plains of Kansas. That kind of entrenched, well-funded, and well-organized competition is very difficult to disrupt.

Still, craft beer's influence is growing every year.

According to the Brewers Association, a Boulder, Colorado–based industry trade group for US independent craft brewers, craft beer sales grew 17.2 percent in 2013 even as the overall beer market shrunk by 1.9 percent. Production by microbreweries, brewpubs, contract brewers, and regional brewers has more than tripled since 2004, reaching an astonishing 15 million barrels in 2013. That's equivalent to 465 million gallons of beer, all produced by US workers at independent breweries in cities and towns across the country.

Given the fact that craft beer is an agricultural product that, in most cases, needs to be consumed within a few months of production, regional breweries and small-time operations have blossomed in this market, peddling locally sourced products and serving their communities directly with fresh beer in casual, informal settings. These small, startup brewers are truly the heart of the local craft beer scene, bringing fresh recipes, fresh styles, and fresh energy to neighborhoods nationwide, both in the form of tiny nano operations as well as larger, better-funded brewpubs and tasting rooms. And, as with all manufacturing businesses, it all starts with the product.

"You've got to make a good product first and foremost," says Matt Simpson, a.k.a. The Beer Sommelier, a craft beer industry consultant. "You can't take the product for granted. Quality is never a given."

The prefix *nano* indicates "one billionth part of something," according to Merriam-Webster's dictionary, and is derived from the Greek word for *dwarf*. This makes sense when considering terms like nanometer, nanoparticle, and nanosecond—all science and engineering concepts generally associated with units of time or length. It also appears in math as a unit prefix denoting 0.000000001 or 10^{-9}. In short, a nano version of anything is tiny, a sliver of a sliver of a sliver.

That doesn't necessarily hold true when speaking of nanobreweries, however. They are small operations, true—though not infinitesimally, mathematically small like nanoparticles—but the spirit of the term holds true, and the message remains clear: these are tiny, self-contained breweries. No bells, whistles, or flashy, corporate operations here.

The fact is, a hard-and-fast rule as to what signifies a "nanobrewery" does not exist. The closest you'll likely get comes from the Brewer's Association, which simply defines craft brewing operations as "small, independent and traditional"— nanos themselves are not specifically addressed. For craft brewers overall, however, this definition effectively boils down to an annual production of between 15,000 and 6,000,000 barrels of beer, at least 75 percent ownership from outside the established alcoholic beverage industry, and beer production that focuses on flavor from both traditional and innovative brewing ingredients. That's a craft brewer. Microbreweries are further defined by the organization as those that meet all of the above criteria but produce fewer than 15,000 barrels per year. (And, just to get one confusing aspect of this out of the way immediately, the use of the word *microbrew* has changed since the 1980s, when the term referred to everything that we now know as *craft beer*. Today's microbrewers are simply smaller craft brewers.)

So, in that sense, nanobreweries are effectively just microbreweries. Very, very small microbreweries, often (but not always) working on three-barrel or smaller brewhouse systems and generally (but not always) only serving their beers through their own taprooms, not via distribution or bottling. They're making very little beer, very well. In this book, I profile a number of small brewers, some of which are nanos, some of which are not, and the definition certainly gets hazy. But the fact is, there's more to neighborhood brewing than just size and scale.

For the record, 6 million barrels of beer on the high end of craft brewing is a lot of beer, and the vast majority of breweries that most of us would consider "craft" produce far, far fewer than that. In fact, the largest craft brewery in the country in terms of annual production as of 2015 was The Boston Beer Company, the maker of Samuel Adams Boston Lager, and it produces just 4.4 million barrels per year on average. Sierra Nevada Brewing ranks second on that list with just over 1 million barrels of production as of the end of 2014. Only one other craft brewer even cracks the million-barrel mark as of this writing, and that's New Belgium Brewing in Fort Collins, Colorado. Every other independent brewer, including some well-known national names, produces fewer.

Compare that to the global beer industry leaders, however, and it quickly becomes clear how far behind the craft industry is. AB InBev sold roughly 45.4 million barrels of Bud Light in 2011 and 16 million barrels of Budweiser in 2014 (though that was down sharply from its 50-million-barrel peak in 1988). Coors Light overtook the "King of Beers" in 2011 as the second most popular beer in America with 18.2 million barrels sold that year. By any measure, these numbers are staggering and prove how much room craft beer still has to grow.

So where does that leave the nanobrewers? At the moment, they're in a little bit of limbo. They're small, yes, and they produce less beer than most of their competitors. But nanobrewing isn't just about being small. It isn't only about production numbers and seating capacity. It is a unique business and beverage model all its own. So what other defining characteristics separate these nanos from the larger microbrewing community?

One key differentiator is the hardware used. The generally accepted rule is that a nanobrewery is a commercial operation based on no more than a three-barrel system, capable of brewing roughly ninety-three gallons at a time. Compare that to the typical five-gallon homebrewing system and you can see these are generally just amped-up homebrew operations. A typical commercial brewery or brewpub is based on a ten-barrel system.

Of course, plenty of exceptions to this rule exist. For example, the Coney Island Brewing Company operated on a one-gallon brewing system, earning it the recognition of being the "smallest commercial brewery in the world," according to the Guinness Book of World Records, before shutting down in 2012. (It was actually a side project owned by the Shmaltz Brewing Company, the maker of the HE'BREW line of craft beers.) On the flip side, Kalispell Brewing Company in northern Montana is still considered a nano despite its ten-barrel system, ticking off a lot of other boxes as a locally focused, flavor-first kind of brewer. In practice, these smaller systems—and even a ten-barrel system qualifies as small among most commercial breweries—mean that, to produce enough beer to meet their needs, the staff must brew more often than larger operators. At Kalispell, for instance, the brew staff is able to produce roughly 310 gallons of beer, at 31 gallons per barrel, on its ten-barrel system each time it brews. That's enough to supply its taproom, but for the business to reach its stated goal of 710 barrels per year, the brewhouse has to be cranking at least every five days, year-round.

As a general rule, most nanobreweries currently fall into a few different categories, as defined by ProBrewer.com, an industry web forum. Sometimes they are simply proof of concept operations, first steps into the industry by brewers who may have larger commercial aspirations but aren't yet sure they have a strong market for their beers. One example of this model in action in Colorado is Crooked Stave, a wild- and sour-beer focused brewery in Denver that started off on a small nano system in an industrial park in 2010 (after moving that operation from Fort Collins) before moving to a far larger and more accessible facility in the heart of the city's entertainment district a couple years later. The second common type of nanobrewer, according to ProBrewer.com, is the add-on brewery, a house-brewed beers program that's simply added on to an existing restaurant or pub. Finally, the "hobby gone wild" model has become increasingly common in the market in recent years. These are often founded by dedicated homebrewers who want to share their product with a small group of faithful fans and participate in the commercial space as a second income source without giving up their primary career. Think of it as a part-time brewery.

"So where does that leave nanobrewing? Basically as a foot in the door," writes Patrick Emerson, an associate professor of economics at Oregon State University, on his *Oregon Economics Blog*. "If there is intense enough local demand for craft beer and enough beer nuts out there who will go off in search of nanobrews, some local bottle shops and pubs that will serve nanobrews, and a robust enough demand to be able to charge premium prices, then I suppose it can be a way to try and build up some funds to pay for future expansion. . . . Nanobreweries are just a stepping stone—even those who think they will remain small, will soon find the tide of economic forces carrying them along."

The truth is, nanobrewing is about attitude as much as anything else, and that's the approach to the subject that I take in this book. I spoke to many brewers who were working on systems larger than the proverbial three-barrel nano system but still fit my general definition of a neighborhood brewery—small, local, independent, and community-focused—and I spoke with plenty of true nanobrewers who were vastly different from the stereotypical "hobbyist" brewer, finding success on their own terms and via their own unique business models. There is no silver bullet when it comes to this category.

Overall, though, the brewers profiled in this book are here because they're focusing their businesses and their livelihoods on creativity, flavor, and adventurous approaches to beer. No matter how big or small they (technically) are, they want to remain involved with their communities and the customers they serve. They want to bring quality products to people who appreciate them as much as they do, and they're willing to stay small (and often closer to the line in terms of revenue and profitability) to do that. Whether they're reworking historic beer styles (like wheatgrass and lemon Hefeweizens, or regulation German-style lagers based on American ingredients), introducing strange new ingredients (doughnut-infused stouts, for example), or simply creating entirely new styles of their very own, the business model is up to them. They're the bosses; as customers, the rest of us are just along for the ride.

And that's kind of the point.

"One of the advantages is that you're not limited," Joel Mahaffey, the cofounder of Foundation Brewing in Portland, Maine, told *Paste* magazine about nanobrewing in the spring of 2015. "Everything is on a small scale, so you're not locked into one style of brewing. I think that's always going to be a struggle for us, actually, to make sure that we don't wander too far off the path, because we really love trying different things. As a brewery, that's something we really love doing in the tasting room—doing smaller batches of stuff. That's one thing that keeps our customers coming back. They love our regular beers of course, but they like to see what we've been up to in the last few weeks, and the tasting room is a good venue for that."

The fact of the matter is that, unlike most other alcoholic beverage providers, local breweries are small businesses. These are not giant, faceless corporations. These are real human beings serving the beer they make almost directly out of their brewhouses. They're part of their local communities, they're friends, they're neighbors, and they aren't in business to make the next Corona Light or Heineken that appeals to everyone and is available everywhere. These are brewers who have dedicated their lives to crafting and perfecting a time-honored product, to serving good stuff to their neighbors, and to generally remaining as independent and free from outside influence as they can. And, at this small scale, they're more able to brew what they personally want to drink, even taking chances on strange styles or different types of ingredients.

Writes the Brewers Association: "When trying to define craft beer, each beer lover has a unique interpretation and story of discovery to share. To make a true craft beer definition even more difficult, each individual beer brand is one of a kind."

CHAPTER 2

AMERICA'S FAVORITE DRINK

"Beer, if drunk in moderation, softens the
temper, cheers the spirit, and promotes health."
—Thomas Jefferson

*I*t's hot in here, and getting hotter.

That's one thing they never tell you about brewing beer; it isn't a party, it's cooking. It's work—true, manual labor kind of work—and doing this day in and day out requires not just a dedication to the product but a love of the process, as well. And that's why many professional brewers do this. They love it. They love the challenge of brewing at scale, the creativity that goes into the recipes and the flavors, and the process of making beer in all of its flexible, roll-with-the-punches glory. They *want* to be here, lifting these sacks of grain and watching these steaming pots for hours.

It's also a hot and sticky process, starting with gallons upon gallons of boiling water and steeping for more than an hour. Humidity is to be expected, along with sweat.

I first visited the brewhouse at Grandma's House, an independent brewery on the southern outskirts of downtown Denver, Colorado, in early Spring. In what had once been an antique shop's storefront, owner Matthew Fuerst had carved out his own piece of Colorado's burgeoning small beer market, complete with a seven-barrel brewing system, a small-but-growing distribution program, and a taproom out front. The space was huge; easily less than half was being used for the taproom and brewhouse operations, giving Feurst plenty of room to expand down the road if he needed to. Not only did he have more than 1,000 square feet of extra space in the brewery for additional fermenters and barrel storage, but also a gigantic 3,000-square-foot space in the middle of the building, complete with a mezzanine level on all three sides, that could be converted into extra bar or restaurant seating if needed.

We talked in the back room as we waited for the shiny—stainless steel mash tun to heat up so we could start the mashing process—the first stage in all-grain brewing in which the barley and other grains are hydrated with hot water, steeping for up to 90 minutes until they leave behind a starch-heavy tea that contains the fermentable sugars needed to convert the liquid into alcohol. His mash tun stood roughly five feet tall and could hold more than 200 gallons of water. Once the mash is complete, the heated grains are "lautered," a washing process that separates the grains from the liquid wort, which is pumped out and boiled in the next step in the process. First, the existing wort is removed from the mash tun and, depending on the brewer's preference, recycled through the grains to pull out any remaining moisture. Then, the entire grain bill is sparged with clean, hot water to bring the total amount of liquid wort up to whatever level the brewer needs for their system (in this case, a total of 220 gallons or seven barrels' worth). The soaked grains—known as "spent grain" at this point—are then removed from the process and discarded; sometimes this material is donated to local farmers who use the leftovers in their livestock feed.

Wort is a strange thing. It looks and smells a lot like beer, but in terms of taste, it's still nowhere near what most people would consider to be a drinkable product. At this point, you're really looking at more of a sweet, malted grain tea. Real beer doesn't exist until yeast has been introduced to the mix and given time to consume the sugars in the wort, thereby creating alcohol and altering the flavor profile via its own adjuncts.

At Grandma's House, all of this takes place in what was once the loading dock of the antique store, facing out to the alley behind an oversized garage door. There, the brewers start each session—which was happening about once a week when I first met Fuerst but ramped up steadily in the months following the opening—by thoroughly and intensely cleaning every surface, kettle, and tool involved in the process, scrubbing everything with a mixture of chemical sterilizers. Homebrewers know this part of the process well. Unsterilized equipment is the most common hurdle for novice brewers because it allows microscopic amounts of bacteria into the beer that can ruin the flavor and drinkability of the final product. And it doesn't take a chemist to explain why this happens. After boiling, raw beer sits at roughly room temperature, depending on the style, for several weeks as it goes through the fermentation process, giving any bacteria present in the mix more than enough time to wreak havoc on the final product. Hence, a clean brewhouse is paramount.

"Cleanliness is the foremost concern of the brewer," writes John J. Palmer in his classic guide to homebrewing, *How to Brew.* "Providing good growing conditions for the yeast in the beer also provides good growing conditions for other microorganisms, especially wild yeast and bacteria. Cleanliness must be maintained through every stage of the brewing process."

The key to avoiding this fate is brutally cleaning every surface that will come into contact with the beer, from the inside of the cook pots to the spoons and spatulas used to stir the mixture as it boils. Even the storage tanks where the fermentation process will take place get a thorough cleaning between uses in case any free-flying contaminants have found their way in after the previous batch was pumped out.

Palmer breaks down this process into three levels: clean, sanitize, and sterilize. At the first level, all equipment and materials used in the brewing process must be free of dirt, stains, and foreign matter. Sanitizing takes this a step further, reducing any microorganisms present to "negligible levels," either by killing them or washing them away with soaps and cleaning solutions. Sterilization takes it all the way, eliminating all forms of life by "chemical or physical means." The reality, he says, is that full sterilization is not required for most brewing operations, particularly homebrewers, and the same holds true at the commercial level. This isn't open-heart surgery; sanitizing to reduce contaminants to negligible levels is enough to prevent most potential spoiling issues.

Once the lautering process is complete, the wort is boiled for roughly sixty to ninety minutes, removing excess water from the mix and raising the specific gravity, or relative water density, of the wort. Brewers measure this figure throughout the beer-making process, using a tool called a hydrometer, to track the progress of fermentation and the development of the beer. Alcohol formation by yeast lowers the overall gravity of the mixture because ethanol is less dense than water. When the specific gravity stops falling, it's an indication that fermentation has finished. Every recipe, then, starts with an original gravity reading and a final gravity reading.

During the boil, hops are added at specific intervals to flavor the final beer and to act as a preservative. They're added early on for depth of flavor and then again, later, for bitterness and aroma, often several times. Some recipes even call for dried hops to be added at the very end of the boil to maximize the bitter flavors they bring. And it's not just about hops at this stage. Fruits, spices, vegetables, and a wide range of other flavoring and coloring agents can be added to the mix during and immediately after the boil, depending on the style of beer the brewer wants to make, allowing the sugars in those ingredients and those extracted from the grains time to break down into the wort.

At Grandma's House, a brewhouse software system monitors and controls all this and can adjust all the temperatures in the system in real time, ensuring that each step lasts just as long as it should and that all water levels and temperatures stay right where they need to be. It also helps to keep the brewer honest, ensuring that each of their hop additions happens on schedule.

Once the boil stage is finished, the wort is pumped out of the brew kettle and into a fermentation tank, a cylindrical stainless steel vessel where the yeast will be added and the beer will be stored as it goes through the fermentation process, which typically lasts a week or two. At commercial breweries, liquid brewers' yeast is pitched into the fermenter at this point to start the process, and from then on, the process is effectively out of the hands of the brewery staff; the yeast does the heavy lifting of converting the wort's sugars into alcohol. Once fermented, the final step in the process is carbonation, most often done at the commercial level via forced CO_2 injection (just like soda or sparkling water). Although, the traditional method of cask fermentation via the addition of excess sugar at the end of the process has become popular amongst craft brewers in recent years, as it brings a unique flavor and mouthfeel to the finished product.

And that, at least technically, is all there is to it.

But for an independent brewer like Grandma's House, the actual process of making the beer is just the start of the story. The real work begins once the kegs are filled and the doors are opened.

When I first set out to profile the ultra-small craft brewing movement—these nanobreweries, as they're called, as well as neighborhood brewers—I expected to learn a little something about the brewing process, maybe use those skills to improve my own homebrew efforts, and perhaps figure out what makes the modern beer business unique and interesting in its own right. I also expected to drink some good beer, get to know the workers behind the scenes in the industry, and learn more about what brings people into this line of work in the first place. It was to be a business book, a look at a growing industry from the inside out.

What I didn't expect was just how much the reality of life at a commercial brewery would differ from my expectations.

When you're brewing on a five- or six-gallon system, as most homebrewers and novice beer hobbyists do, you gain an understanding of the basic building blocks of beer and some experience working through the entire process from start to finish, albeit at a small scale. You learn how to prepare the equipment, how long to mash the grains, how to strain and separate the wort, how much water to add before pitching your yeast, and most importantly, how to choose the correct ingredients and techniques to make the beer style you want to make.

At an industrial scale, even the comparatively small scale of a nanobrewer, many of those experiences and expectations can get complicated—and expensive. When you're brewing multiple times per week, and that's typical for even the smallest of small-time commercial operators, a lot of the nitpicky decisions that are part of homebrewing—what type of malt to use, when to pitch the yeast, how often to add the hops—become critical and time-sensitive business decisions. Too much is at stake to risk screwing up a batch, from the financial success of the business to the taste of the beer itself. Everything has to be standardized, from the ingredients to the recipes to the timing and production schedules. There simply isn't enough time in the day to mull over yeast strain choices and malt crush sizes, especially when you're working to ensure consistency across barrels and batches.

That's not to say that commercial brewers are timid when it comes to experimentation—far from it, in fact, and we'll explore that part of the business in depth in a later chapter. The truth is there has to be a structure in place to ensure a quality, consistent brew time and time again. Most brewers aren't firing from the hip; they are developing recipes, dialing in the flavors they want, and then putting systems in place to ensure they can execute on those recipes every time. It's a business of spreadsheets, schedules, and production planning, of washing kegs, unloading grain shipments, negotiating with ingredient suppliers, and repairing industrial equipment. It's heavy, manual labor that at times feels more like an assembly line than a mad scientist's workshop, given the step-by-step and procedural nature of the work itself.

In short, this is American manufacturing with a modern twist.

Think about that the next time you sit down to an experimental brew at your favorite taproom. Yes, grapefruit IPA is an interesting twist on the standard India Pale Ale flavor, but the brewer had a lot at stake when they first put that recipe together and started the process that resulted in that beer. They likely perfected the recipe on a small pilot system, sourced just the right ingredients from their suppliers, compared various batches to dial in the flavor they wanted, and codified the process so that their brewers know what they're creating and how to get there next time. None of this is an accident.

And that, in reality, is the story of this book: craft brewing as a new type of heavy industry, one that combines art, engineering, flavor, marketing, investment capital, and more to create a functional business.

This couldn't be happening at a better time either. Manufacturing in the United States has been on a downward spiral for more than three decades due in part to new competition from China and increases in productivity and automation across all sorts of different industries. The 2000s were especially rough for the manufacturing sector, resulting in the loss of about 5.8 million American jobs, or one-third of the country's manufacturing workforce, according to the US Bureau of Labor Statistics. In 1979, the peak of US manufacturing employment, some 19.5 million Americans worked in manufacturing-related jobs, accounting for 12.5 percent of the working population at that time. And they were well paid, too. On an inflation-adjusted basis, the median household income in those days for high school graduates who had no further education was just over $56,000 per year (in 2013 dollars), according to the Census Bureau. That figure peaked in 1973 and has been declining ever since.

Compare that to today. The manufacturing sector now employs about 12.3 million Americans, or about 4.5 percent of the population, a 37-percent decline since 1979. Household income for many of these workers is down sharply, as well, at just over $40,000 per year as of 2013, representing an inflation-adjusted drop of nearly $16,000, or 27.8 percent, for non-college graduates since the early 1970s.

The decline in the US manufacturing sector has been about more than just jobs. The economy as a whole has suffered, argue Adams Nager and Robert Atkinson of the Information Technology and Innovation Foundation, both in terms of reduced consumer spending as well as a reduction in overall exports for the country. In their January 2015 report, "The Myth of America's Manufacturing Renaissance: The Real State of U.S. Manufacturing," Nager and Atkinson write:

"In the 2000s, American manufacturing experienced the steepest losses in employment in American history and serious decline in output. These were caused in no small way by a significant worsening of the manufacturing goods trade deficit, which was $458 billion in 2013. Additionally, trade in advanced technology products, which in 1990 represented a $35 billion trade surplus for the United States, became a deficit in 2002 and has since declined even further, becoming an $81 billion deficit by 2013.

"Between 2000 and 2009, America's manufacturing sector shed 33.6 percent of its jobs (approximately 5.8 million), a 40.1 percent decline when controlling for the fact that the overall workforce grew. To compare, in the 1990s, the United States lost only 3 percent of manufacturing jobs. Yet, manufacturing productivity growth rates were more or less the same in both decades.

"When measured properly, manufacturing output also experienced significant decline in the 2000s. From 2000 to 2009, real manufacturing value added officially grew by 7.7 percent. Over the same time, however, GDP grew by 14.7 percent, meaning that manufacturing was in a state of relative decline compared to the rest of the economy."

Yes, it has been a bad few decades for the skilled trades in this country. But, as Tesla founder Elon Musk has said, "The rumours of the demise of the U.S. manufacturing industry are greatly exaggerated." Why is Musk so optimistic? Because, as traditional American manufacturing industries like steel production and textiles have declined, new twenty-first-century players have stepped in to take their places.

Musk's electric car maker Tesla is a good example; not only does the company employ thousands of US workers to build its cars at its southern California assembly plant, but it is also in the process of developing new battery technology for home and auto use and will be manufacturing those domestically, as well. And Tesla is not alone. Onshoring, the practice of bringing jobs back to the US from overseas, has been in vogue among domestic firms in recent years, particularly in terms of IT, finance, and business services functions, as companies look to take advantage of lower labor costs in parts of this country (particularly smaller cities) as well as tax incentives and the benefits of proximity to both headquarters and customers.

In manufacturing, however, the onshoring shift has been slower to take hold. For instance, in 2013, Apple announced a $100 million plan to start manufacturing some of its Mac computers in this country and bankrolled two domestic plants—one in Mesa, Arizona, and another in Austin, Texas—as well as a repair facility in Pennsylvania.

"We are proud to expand our domestic manufacturing initiative with a new facility in Arizona, creating more than 2,000 jobs in engineering, manufacturing, and construction," Apple spokeswoman Kristin Huguet told CNET at the time. "This new plant will make components for Apple products and it will run on 100 percent renewable energy from day one, as a result of the work we are doing with SRP to create green energy sources to power the facility."

The plan sputtered, however, by 2014 when Apple's production partner, GT Advanced Technologies, declared bankruptcy and the iPhone maker was forced to convert its 1.3 million-square-foot Arizona facility into a data center. The company does still manufacture its Mac Pro desktop systems in Texas, though not at the scale originally planned.

But there are still success stories out there that illustrate the return-to-manufacturing trend in action, and the small-time craft beverages movement is one of them. No, brewers (and craft distillers) are nowhere near the level of replacing the domestic auto industry as a component of US gross domestic product, but the rise of nanobrewing and craft food and beverage in recent years is indicative of a larger, perhaps more powerful, trend in US society: the desire on the part of many Americans to make things again. We want to create, to build, to sit down at the end of the day with a physical product in our hands that we can point to and say, "I did that."

In many ways, this is a reaction to the technology that has come to define not only much of our working lives but modern culture in general. For plenty of Americans in 2016, if we aren't sitting at our desk for nine hours every day peering at a computer screen, we're focusing on our smartphone during the commute, tapping on our tablet at home, or sitting on the couch just watching TV, a more "traditional" type of electronic screen. Many people have grown tired of this reality and are looking for ways to reconnect with the physical world—the exponential growth of Etsy, the online marketplace for handmade crafts, is just one example of this desire in action. Gross sales for Etsy sellers in 2014 totaled more than $1.9 billion, up 56 percent from the year before, and that has manifested itself in the rise of the do-it-yourself (DIY) movement.

Craft food and beverage is a big part of this overall trend.

According to the Beer Institute, the brewing, distribution, and retail sale of beer (including both craft and non-craft producers) generates about $6.9 billion in economic activity in Colorado, supporting about 22,000 jobs directly and another 35,000 when support industries such as agriculture, real estate, transportation, business services, and others are taken into account. As a whole, the industry pays out more than $3 billion in annual wages to workers here and pays some $2.5 billion in federal, state, and local taxes in the state every year. As of 2014, Colorado ranked third in the country for breweries and brewpubs per capita with 235 total craft brewing operations producing more than 1.6 million barrels of beer (or 13.6 gallons per adult in the state) every year. And growth? As of 2011, there were only 126 breweries statewide. That figure has nearly doubled in just over four years.

In the state capital of Denver—Colorado's largest city—the brewery explosion has been even more dramatic, jumping from just a handful in the metro area less than a decade ago to dozens and dozens today. And new outfits are opening all the time; it's often not a question of whether to go to a new craft brewery opening on a given weekend, but a question of *which one*? The variety is staggering, too. We have brewers, both nanos and larger, that specialize in cask-conditioned English-style ales, German biergarten lagers, organic-only ingredients, specialty and niche flavors (like seasonal ales brewed with watermelon or peaches), and many more. We have brewpubs that serve food with their beers, standalone tasting rooms focusing strictly on the beer in a TV-free environment, and even single-barrel breweries built into warehouse spaces in industrial parts of the city where customers sip in what look and feel like converted garages. Some brewers focus on Belgian-style saisons and farmhouse ales, some strictly brew red ales, some only stouts and dark beers. The city even has a craft brewery focused entirely on sour beers, a distinct European style that was all but nonexistent in this country until a few years ago. Every neighborhood in the city (almost) has its own nanobrewery at this point with, as of 2014, experts estimating between 80 and 100 taprooms with on-site production were operating within the city limits. Of those, the majority would qualify as nanobrewing operations, brewing their beers on-site, on a small brewhouse system, and selling directly to customers at their own taproom.

Colorado's business-friendly regulatory climate gets some of the credit for this rapid expansion. Under current licensing terms, breweries are able to operate on-site taprooms without having to jump through too many regulatory hurdles (e.g., registering as a full restaurant or food service provider and paying the associated fees). This allows brewers, and particularly new brewers who are working under tight cost pressures, to set up shop effectively as standalone bars and bypass many of the food-and-beverage oversight laws that would add additional requirements to their startup costs. The flip side of this is the limitation that brewers can only sell their own beers out of their tasting rooms and can't operate kitchens to serve food. Moving into either of those areas, as some nanobrewers have done in recent years, requires a shift to full brewpub status for regulatory purposes, meaning commercial kitchen requirements, new licensing, and other hoops to jump through.

"The idea of market saturation had crossed our mind," Sarah Howat, who co-owns the Former Future Brewing Company in Denver with her husband James (opening their shop in 2013 with a 3.5-barrel brewing system), told the Denver Business Journal in 2014. "But you never hear someone say, 'this neighborhood is oversaturated with restaurants,' even though if I go from one restaurant to the next a lot of them serve the same products, the same liquor, the same beer. With craft beer, you can't get my beer anywhere else."

And Howat is not alone in this view of the marketplace. At a 2013 roundtable discussion on the future of craft beer in Colorado sponsored by the *Denver Post*, Bill Eye, the head brewer of Prost Brewing (which crafts traditional pilsners, lagers, and other German-style beers at its taproom and facility on the city's north side) asked: "Why can't there be a brewery on every corner, like there is a dive bar on every corner?" (It's worth noting, however, that Prost is no nanobrewer, operating on a seventy-barrel brewing system acquired from a shuttered brewery in Bamberg, Germany, and shipped to Colorado, piece by piece. Glittering in copper and steel, it is a sight to behold.)

These brewery taprooms are all stand-alone brands, selling their own products, but there remains, in the view of many, more than enough market to go around, just as there is for bars. These are the new neighborhood pubs, the new gathering spots. This is a proliferation of very local options—all producing very good products, but hardly destinations in their own right—and that fact is key to the long-term success of many craft brewers working at this small scale. Good beer is good beer, and you'd be hard-pressed to find a craft brewer that isn't making good beer at this point. But good beer at a taproom that's five minutes from home? That you can walk to? That's something that most neighborhoods are still proving happy to support.

But none of this is to say that it's just a Colorado thing. Quite the contrary, in fact. Although a number of what I call craft brewing "regions" exist across the country—hotbeds like Washington, California, and Wisconsin—craft brewing, at the nano scale and beyond, is happening in small towns and big cities from coast to coast. In fact, independent operations are popping up all over, from Great Lakes Brewing in Cleveland, Devils Backbone Brewing in Virginia's Shenandoah Valley, and the single-beer brewery, The Alchemist, maker of the award-winning and coveted Heady Topper, in Waterbury, Vermont.

And that's just scratching the surface of this trend. According to ProBrewer.com, as of 2014, roughly three hundred breweries operated in the United States that qualifed as nanos, accounting for about 10 percent of all craft breweries at that point. The total selection of craft breweries includes 1,871 "micro" breweries; 1,412 brewpubs (where beer is brewed on the premises and served alongside food); and 135 regional breweries. They are all part of what was a $246.5 billion industry in the United States as of 2012 that, including macrobrewers, employs more than 2 million people and generates some $49 billion in business, personal, and consumption taxes.

This is truly a national story.

In the decades since craft brewing really took off in this country, the market for these beverages has grown and evolved dramatically, from a small-time niche interest to becoming a real threat to the incumbent beer industry. And, especially at the nano scale, these aren't mass-produced, mass-marketed products. They're handmade, one-batch-at-a-time drinks. No fancy bells and whistles—just high-quality, flavorful beer.

And they are starting to make the incumbents nervous.

CHAPTER 3

HOW DID WE GET HERE?

"He was a wise man who invented beer."
—Plato

*I*t all started with the ancient Mesopotamians.

That's the generally accepted story about beer's history, right? Brewed beverages, they say, were first developed in the Fertile Crescent region at roughly the same time as bread, becoming a key part of the diet of many ancient peoples, including the Egyptians, Babylonians, Assyrians, and others.

How this all came together is certainly simple enough. Wild yeast most likely found its way into some of the sugar-laden liquids early humans created as soon as they domesticated grains. The yeast did its work, which at the time was largely a mystery, and the end result was the first fermented beverage. It probably happened more or less by accident and, given that wild yeasts are effectively everywhere, likely took hold in civilizations all over the world at roughly the same time. (Wine, for example, went through a similar creation cycle as fermented grape juices appeared in many different civilizations at roughly the same time thanks to the near-universal presence of wild yeast.)

The oldest hard evidence of the practice of brewing beer is a Sumerian tablet from the fifth century BCE depicting a group sharing a drink from a wide, low vessel outfitted with straws, the traditional way groups enjoyed beer in those days. A poem from the same culture took it a step further some two thousand years later by introducing to history what is considered the oldest recorded recipe for beer, included as part of a description of the brewing process that was dedicated to Ninkasi, the Sumerian goddess of brewing.

But that's just the hard evidence. Scientists have proven the practice of brewing itself dates back even further, finding evidence of brewed beer on pottery jars found in Iran that date back some seven thousand years. Beer is, to put it mildly, one of the oldest beverages in human history and one of our first food- and drink-related creations as a people. It's one of those things that cultures all over the world have in common.

"Humankind was built on beer," writes William Bostwick, the beer critic for the *Wall Street Journal,* in his 2014 book, *The Brewer's Tale: A History of the World According to Beer.* "From the world's first writing to its first laws, in rituals social, religious and political, civilization is soaked in beer. Some historians even think that beer gave us the crucial vitamins and nutrients—not to mention a source of purified water—to keep us healthy as we turned from meat-centric nomads to a settled, agrarian diet. Beer was foundational stuff, a building block of human existence."

But let's first clarify what we mean when we use the word *beer* in the context of these ancient civilizations. The beers these early brewers were creating all over the world were most likely created using the same basic methods: a sugar solution was mixed into water and then left to sit out for a period of time, allowing the wild yeast to handle the fermentation and turn the mixture into a primitive beer, which likely seemed like magic in those days. But that's where the similarities end. True, yeast can turn just about any sugar source into alcohol, but beer differed from culture to culture in those days, depending on the local ingredients brewers in each area had access to.

Professor Linda Raley from Texas Tech University explained it best in her 1998 work, "A Concise Timeline of Beer History." Egyptian brewers were known to use barley in their beers, as we do today, she wrote, although other Africans also used the various other grains they had access to, including millet, maize, and cassava, in their beers. In South America, corn was used to create the sugar solution, whereas persimmon and agave were more common among North American civilizations. Japanese brewing was based around rice, resulting in what we now know as sake, though brewers in other parts of Asia used sorghum, a type of wild grass, and wheat at times. All these qualify as beer, in terms of the processes that went into making them, but they were very different products at the end of the day.

Granted, most modern beer drinkers would be hard-pressed to identify what these ancient brewers were making as "beer." Homebrewer Horst Dornbusch researched these ancient recipes to make his Pharaoh Ale, describing it for the American Homebrewers Association's *New Brewer* magazine this way:

"The Pharaoh ale tasted unlike any other brew, in part because our modern palates have become so accustomed to the presence of hops. The brew has a minimal but fresh and appetizing bouquet. Visually, it is slightly turbid, and the color is deep reddish amber to almost light mahogany. The up-front taste shows mild notes of nuttiness (probably from the dates), with a faint scent of rose petals and perhaps of almond extract—probably a contribution from the mandrake root tea. The body is medium. As the brew spreads over the palate, strong malty notes as well as a definite date and honey aroma take over, which is especially noticeable because of the absence of any hop bitterness. This is a surprise but not an obstacle. The brew also takes on mild, lingering herb-like notes, which only serve to enhance its drinkability."

Different, to say the least.

Delaware craft brewer Dogfish Head Brewery has made a business out of these long-lost recipes via its Ancient Ales series of specialty brews, which it has been creating since 1999 in partnership with Dr. Patrick McGovern, a professor of anthropology at the University of Pennsylvania Museum in Philadelphia and the self-described "Indiana Jones of Ancient Ales, Wines, and Extreme Beverages." The first beer in the series, named Midas Touch and based on molecular evidence found in what is believed to be the tomb of King Midas in Turkey, is a slightly "sweet yet dry beer made with honey, barley malt, white muscat grapes, and saffron." It is also the most award-winning beer the brewer has created to date. In addition, they have brewed a drink called Chateau Jiahu based on a 9,000-year-old recipe found in a tomb in China, believed to be history's first known fermented beverage; Theobroma, a brew made from cocoa, honey, chilies, and annatto and based on remnants of the beverage found on 3,400-year-old pottery found in Honduras; Birra Etrusca Bronze, a 2,800-year-old Italian recipe for a barley- and wheat-based beer, and several others. Their Kvasir is based on a 3,500-year-old Dutch recipe and made of lingonberries, cranberries, myrica gale, yarrow, honey, and birch syrup, while their Sah'tea is made from rye, juniper, and chai tea in the style of tenth-century Finland. By brewing these ancient recipes, Dogfish Head jokes that it "just might be the most traditional modern brewery in the world."

The point is that beer can be made with just about anything.

All this proves, though, is that brewed beverages are, on the whole, a pretty straightforward product. You boil some water, add some malted cereal grains (or whatever else you have sitting around), and let it all steep over low heat until it turns into a starchy, sweetened liquid: tea, essentially. This is your raw beer, what we now call wort, no matter if you're brewing with barley, rice, or persimmon. The brewer then strains out the solids, adds in any aromatics and flavoring agents they want to use (these days that usually means hops), pitches in a measure of yeast to start the fermentation, and then lets it all hang out together for a few weeks while the yeast converts the sugars in the wort into alcohol.

Then you drink it.

That's pretty much all there is to it; it's easy. The ancient Egyptians did it that way, Babylonian King Hammurabi codified it this way in the eighteenth century BCE, and the good people at MillerCoors and Anheuser-Busch do it (pretty much) this way today.

Taken in context, then, the so-called Purity Law Germany passed in 1516 (a.k.a. the Reinheitsgebot) to regulate the contents of its beers makes a little more sense. Under the terms of the regulation, to be sold as "beer" in Germany at the time, a beverage had to be made with barley, water, hops, and nothing else (except for wild yeast, of course, which was not yet understood as part of the brewing process at the time). A lot of ambiguity surrounded the brewing of beer in those days, both in terms of ingredients as well as what tavern keepers charged for it, and the German government wanted to protect its citizens from low-quality, overpriced beer. Even now, roughly five hundred years after its creation, the Reinheitsgebot still reads like the dense, legal document that it is:

"Furthermore, we wish to emphasize that in future in all cities, markets and in the country, the only ingredients used for the brewing of beer must be Barley, Hops and Water. Whosoever knowingly disregards or transgresses upon this ordinance, shall be punished by the Court authorities' confiscating such barrels of beer, without fail.

"Should, however, an innkeeper in the country, city or markets buy two or three pails of beer (containing 60 Mass) and sell it again to the common peasantry, he alone shall be permitted to charge one Heller more for the Mass of the Kopf, than mentioned above. Furthermore, should there arise a scarcity and subsequent price increase of the barley (also considering that the times of harvest differ, due to location), WE, the Bavarian Duchy, shall have the right to order curtailments for the good of all concerned."

But the German Purity Law, which has since been lambasted by brewers the world over (Dogfish Head even credits it with the growth of "modern brewing conglomerates" and the "bland lager" they create) was just one part of the development of beer in Europe during this time period. By codifying the rules for what qualified as "beer," government officials were taking steps to standardize what had, for centuries, been a loosely defined product. In early civilizations, beer was made with any number of different ingredients, flavored with an assortment of different spices, resulting in a wide variety of different styles and tastes. That's now the way true, commercial products work.

This approach to brewing continued, however, as beer spread from the ancient cultural centers of the Middle East and Northern Africa to other parts of the world, where it took on more local characteristics. In Europe, where barley and wheat predominated as dietary staples, particular styles and ingredients took hold.

And, this being the Middle Ages, the role of brewer eventually fell to local church officials as the prevailing authority figures of the day. Not only did this help to centralize the production of beer by creating a class of "brewers," it also helped to standardize beer styles and recipes to something that began to resemble the options we know today. Mike Bostwick, the beer critic for the *Wall Street Journal*, explains this period in the history of beer as the "merging of two heritages, Christian and pagan" in his 2014 book, *The Brewer's Tale: A History of the World According to Beer*. Church leaders embraced the beer brewing and drinking traditions of early Europe as a way to win converts to the faith. Not only did they sync up the Christian calendar to align with existing pagan drinking holidays (the feast of Odin became Christmas, for example, and the harvest festival became All Saints Day), but church leaders even embraced beer in their scripture and doctrine.

> "They treated it now with a mix of reverence and humility," Bostwick writes. "Beer was both as wondrous as wine and as commonplace as bread. In Irish lore, Saint Brigit turned water into sacred suds; in some British monasteries beer was penitent enough to drink while fasting. 'Liquida non fragunt ieiunium,' monks said as they sipped— liquid doesn't break the fast. Beer eventually moved from a gesture of acceptance, to—especially during those fasts—a critical piece of church practice. When Saint Benedict decreed in his book of precepts that monasteries following his Benedictine order should welcome passing travelers with food and drink, and that his monks stay self-sufficient, living 'by the labor of their hands,' that work included brewing."

But it was the introduction of hops to beer that really moved brewing from an ancient practice to a modern, commercial product. As we will discuss in chapter 7, hops—or, more specifically, the female flowering cones of the *Humulus lupulus* plant—act as both a flavoring agent in beer as well as a preservative, with an antibacterial effect that prevents unwanted microorganisms from overtaking the yeast in the brew. Hops first came into wide use in brewing in the ninth century, as documented by Hildegard of Bingen, a German Benedictine abbess, but up until that time brewers had been adding all sorts of spices and flavors to their beers in hopes of better preserving them, with little luck. Beer in those days stayed drinkable longer than standing water, but not by much. Not only did the addition of hops help to stabilize the beer so that it would last longer, but the flowers added a pleasant, bitter taste to the final product that balanced well with the headier malt flavors.

"If monastic beer has its foundation in cloistered purity, hopped beer was based on trade," Bostwick writes. "Hops are a much more effective preservative than other traditional spices thanks to a bitter, microbial acid in their flowers called humulone. Beer that kept longer could travel farther, and so hopped-beer brewers could command a wider market than their spice-using competition. Hops also meant that beer could be made weaker and cheaper, with less grain, yet still last as long."

As the popularity of European beers grew, the continent overall emerged as one of the best places on the planet to grow the basic building blocks of beer, including barley and hops, further helping to cement the social status of the drink. So, by the time western explorers began leaving for and reaching the New World, beer was one of their first exports.

Based in a squat, red brick building near the intersection of Mahantongo and Fifth Streets in sleepy Pottsville, Pennsylvania, a coal mining hamlet located about two hours west of Philadelphia and an hour north of Harrisburg, Yuengling & Son carries the distinction of being the oldest continually operating brewing company in the United States, having been established in 1829. It also happens to be one of the largest independent brewers in the country, producing about 2.5 million barrels of beer every year at its three brewing facilities as of 2015, and is tied for first place with The Boston Beer Company, the maker of Samuel Adams Boston Lager, in terms of overall sales by an American-owned brewer.

The family-owned company has come a long way since German immigrant David G. Yuengling (the surname was an Anglicized take on the founder's European surname, Jüngling) moved to Pottsville at twenty-three years of age and started his own brewery, making beers in the traditional German style. The company has since been passed down through the family over the years (current owner Dick Yuengling is the fifth generation in his family to own the operation, having bought it from his father in 1985), and it has seen its share of ups and downs since the nineteenth century, nearly shuttering in the 1970s before experiencing a revival and breakneck growth under current ownership. During Prohibition, for example, Yuengling went into the "near beer" business, brewing low-alcohol versions of its standard offerings, including Yuengling Special, a light lager; Yuengling Por-Tor, a take on their traditional porter; and Yuengling Juno, which was marketed as an early type of energy drink, according to the company.

"It's a tale of shared dreams, individual tenacity and an unwavering dedication to standards of quality," the company's marketing materials read. "Like many American stories it starts amid the dreams of countless young immigrants looking for opportunity and emerges from the strength and will of one family determined to build their legacy in a new country."

Today, Yuengling's beer list includes a traditional lager, an American pilsner, a dark-brewed Baltic porter, a Bock, an Oktoberfest special, a hoppy ale, and light versions of both the lager and the standard pilsner. The company also offers a ready-to-drink black and tan variety, which is a mixture of its porter and pilsners. Its original brewhouse in Pottsville was placed on both the national and state of Pennsylvania historic registers in 1976 and was officially recognized as America's Oldest Brewery that same year.

But just because Yuengling is the oldest doesn't mean it was the first. Far from it, in fact.

Brewing in America dates back to the earliest days of civilization in the region, starting with the corn-based beers Native Americans brewed prior to the European arrival. English and Dutch settlers that reached what is now the East Coast of the United States in the seventeenth century brought their own recipes for beer with them and soon discovered that much of the Eastern seaboard was ideal for the growing of malt and hops and for the brewing of beer in general. By 1660, the city that is now New York, then New Amsterdam, was home to some twenty-six breweries and taverns. Still, in those days, beer was primarily a local product, brewed and served in homes and local taverns throughout the Colonies, but rarely sold further afield, as it did not yet travel well, partly because it was stored in wooden kegs with minimal sterilization or hygiene. That kept the market for beer, which was large and active even then, fairly confined to these local small-time brewers until after the Civil War.

In fact, much of the beer drunk in early American history was what we today would think of more as homebrew than commercial product, and it was a staple of daily life in many households. Founding father George Washington, for instance, was a well-documented beer drinker. He produced it in great quantities for his own family's consumption as well as serving it to guests and staff on a regular basis. Records from his Mount Vernon estate in Virginia show a range of beer-related purchases and details, including the delivery of a wooden cask for aging strong beer in 1761 and a cookbook owned by Martha Washington that included several recipes for beer as well as instructions for "reclaiming" spoiled beer.

"Washington not only drank beer himself and served it to his guests, but it was also one of the items provided for voters when he was a candidate for political office," write the historians at Mount Vernon. "Washington's 1758 election to the House of Burgesses cost him 39 pounds, 6 shillings, a sum, which bought him 'a hogshead and a barrel of punch, thirty-five gallons of wine, forty-three gallons of strong beer, cider, and dinner for his friends.'"

This trend continued both after the Revolutionary War and into Washington's years as president of the new country, during which time he outfitted the executive mansion with a long list of beer-drinking glassware and accessories. Beer supply imports were scarce after the war, however, though it is believed that Washington continued to brew beer at Mount Vernon for "home use," noting to his farm manager in 1793 that, although they would no longer be bottling their beer (presumably due to glass shortages and other supply limitations), "it may be brewed as usual as the occasion requires." Hops were planted on the property in 1785.

Fellow founding father Thomas Jefferson—no slouch to Washington in the alcohol department and a well-known connoisseur of fine wines—was said to have claimed in 1818 that "in nothing have the habits of the palate more decisive influence than in our relish of wines." He tried to plant European grape varieties near his Virginia home to facilitate winemaking, with limited success. He was also a regular beer drinker and even picked up the home-brewing hobby during his retirement from public life in the early nineteenth century as an extension of his scientific interests. According to historians at Monticello, his estate near Charlottesville, Virginia, Jefferson brewed beer personally on at least one occasion in 1812, using locally grown malt and hops, eventually bottling the result.

"For Jefferson and his countrymen, beer was ubiquitous," historians write. "Rural households brewed small quantities in their kitchens for their own use, taverns sold beer to travelers, and in larger cities, established breweries sup-plied the population with malt liquors. The inventory taken after Thomas' father Peter Jefferson's death listed *The London and Country Brewer* among his possessions, suggesting that beer may have been brewed at Shadwell in Jefferson's youth. In the early years of their marriage, Jefferson's wife Martha brewed fifteen-gallon batches of small beer (which has a relatively low alco-holic content) nearly every two weeks. Perhaps with a view toward expanding production, Jefferson's early plans for Monticello's offices (the rooms where household services were carried out) came to include both a brewing room and a beer cellar."

But, as mentioned, beer in those days was a local product out of necessity. It was difficult to ship and nearly impossible to store for any length of time, so as a result, the beer "industry" was extremely scattered and small scale. But beer was becoming increasingly popular just the same, meaning that every hamlet and town across the country needed to have their own brewing operation if they wanted access to the suds, and many of them did just that. In 1810, according to the Brewers Association, there were just 132 breweries across the country. But by 1873, the market's peak, 4,131 US breweries were in operation, and Americans were drinking some 20 gallons of beer per capita annually.

It's often said of today's craft beer resurgence that we now have more breweries in this country than at any time "since Prohibition," and that is technically true. The United States now has more than 3,400 commercial breweries, up more than 19 percent since 2013. But Prohibition wasn't the high-water mark for US brewing; that point came nearly fifty years earlier. The market for beer had been changing long before 1920, when the Eighteenth Amendment to the US Constitution made the "manufacture, sale, or transportation of intoxicating liquors" illegal nationwide. Technological advances, most notably refrigeration and pasteurization, had made the long-distance shipping and storage of beer a reality by the late nineteenth century, negating the need for hyper-local breweries and leading to widespread consolidation in the industry around that same time. By the time alcohol was outlawed nationwide, fewer than one thousand breweries were left in this country.

And the slide only accelerated from there.

Prohibition ended in December 1933 with the passage of the Twenty-first Amendment, which repealed the original act, but the brewers that had survived the 1920s emerged to find a market for their products that was greatly changed. American drinking tastes had shifted to lighter, less bitter lagers, and the industry consolidation that had been underway before 1920 continued to gain steam in the ensuing years, as larger companies gobbled up their smaller rivals. Prohibition not only forced many small, independent brewers out of business, but also effectively created a market in which larger, more diversified brewing companies could thrive, relying on their production efficiencies and sheer scale to corner the market. By 1950, 350 American breweries remained in business, and that number slipped to 188 by 1960. By 1978, only 89 breweries operated in the United States, and most of those were brewing the same type of beer.

"They are pale lager beers vaguely of the pilsener style but lighter in body, notably lacking hop character, and generally bland in palate," British beer critic Michael Jackson wrote of American beers at the time. "They do not all taste exactly the same but the differences between them are often of minor consequence."

But amid all of this consolidation and the dumbing-down of American beer flavors, something else was happening: beer lovers were rediscovering the possibilities of homebrewing, recreating favorite recipes, and otherwise pushing the boundaries of what was possible in what was then a land of light lagers. Belgian sours, English ales, and German Hefeweizens didn't die out during this period; they just went underground. The truth is, were it not for the extended "dark period" of Prohibition, homebrewing would very likely have been a basic life skill in this country (not unlike cooking or sewing) that would have been passed down from generation to generation. Families would have kept their favorite recipes intact, immigrants would have continued brewing the styles they knew from their youth, and Americans would have most likely nurtured a deeper appreciation for beers of all types. We would have known better what we were missing out on. But the Eighteenth Amendment cost us much of this shared experience, and as a result, most of our knowledge of brewing practices died off, only to be rediscovered in the late 1970s.

The homebrewing movement got a significant shot in the arm in 1977 with the passage of House Resolution (HR) 1337, which effectively legalized the practice of homebrewing via a tweak in the tax code. Making beer at home had originally been outlawed as part of the Eighteenth Amendment, but was mistakenly not legalized by the Twenty-first Amendment, which did legalize home winemaking. HR 1337 amended the law to make it legal for Americans to produce beer or wine at home, without paying taxes on it, provided it was not produced for sale.

Per the language of the bill, it was now legal for "any adult to produce wine and beer for personal and family use and not for sale without incurring the wine or beer excise taxes or any penalties for quantities per calendar year of: (1) 200 gallons if there are two or more adults in the household and (2) 100 gallons if there is only one adult in the household."

President Jimmy Carter signed HR 1337 into law on October 14, 1978.

And that was just the first step. Brewpubs were legalized in many states starting in the early 1980s, allowing these now-legal homebrewers to eventually move out of their basements and sell their beers commercially. And a support industry sprung up around them, including homebrewing shops, ingredient suppliers, education programs, and more. This was big. This was new. And this soon began to reshape the beer industry into what we know today. The "craft" side of brewing was going mainstream.

The impact of all these changes was sudden and widespread, leading to, as Charlie Papazian, president of the Brewers Association, describes it, a "democratization of beer," led not by profit-driven corporations but solely by homebrewers and amateur enthusiasts. Some of these brewers eventually opened their own small breweries, some started brewpubs, and others simply continued brewing their favorites at home, working to perfect the art of what was rapidly becoming known as "craft" beer. The truth is, without these efforts to "relearn" how to brew and rediscover forgotten beer styles, the craft revival as we know it today likely never would have happened.

The first brewery to be classified as a "craft brewer" was the Anchor Brewing Company in California, which traces its roots to 1896 when German immigrant Gottleib Brekle moved to San Francisco during the gold rush and began brewing a style of beer known as California Common or Steam Beer. We'll get into the specifics of that particular style in a later chapter, but Steam Beer is brewed with a specific strain of lager yeast that does well at warmer fermentation temperatures than most lager ingredients. In frontier California, where refrigeration was a luxury few could afford, this type of beer proved easy to make and popular to drink. Anchor Brewing went through its own ups and downs throughout the years, eventually moving away from the California Common style to brew more generic American lagers, and was near bankruptcy in 1965 when Frederick Maytag III, the great-grandson of the founder of the Maytag Corporation, bought the brewery with the intention of reviving the steam-style beers that the company had been founded on. His new version of Anchor Steam debuted in bottles in 1971 and, by the 1980s, had become a national sensation—a unique, flavorful beer for a drinking public that had largely forgotten what good beer could taste like.

Anchor Brewing itself became one of the first modern microbreweries, helping to inspire like-minded brewers and entrepreneurs from coast to coast (homebrewers

Ken Grossman and Paul Camusi started Sierra Nevada Brewing Company in Chico, California, in 1979; Boulder Beer got started that same year; and Jim Koch started The Boston Beer Company, the maker of Samuel Adams Boston Lager, in 1984). Bert Grant founded Yakima Brewing & Malting Company in Yakima, Washington, in 1982, making it the country's first brewpub since Prohibition.

Still, it was the 1976 creation of the New Albion Brewing Company in Sonoma, California, that many still speak of with reverence as "the true renaissance of American craft brewing." Founded by Jack McAuliffe, a Silicon Valley engineer by training, the original New Albion didn't last long (it was defunct by 1982), but it left a lasting impression on not only craft beer as a product, but also on many of the people who would go on to create the craft brewing industry as we know it today. As part of the burgeoning "California cuisine" scene of the day, McAuliffe focused his brewery on ingredients, quality, and flavor, brewing bottle-conditioned ales, porters, and stouts on a small, fifty-five-gallon drum–based system of his own design (rumor has it: it was built around two vessels that had once been used to store Coca-Cola syrup McAuliffe had sourced from a nearby bottling plant). Every batch sold out.

Still, it wasn't enough to turn a profit, and McAuliffe was forced to shutter the operation after just six years. His nanobrewing approach left a lasting impression on many in the industry, though, including Sierra Nevada Brewing Company founder Ken Grossman, with whom McAuliffe worked as an early advisor, and many others. Even today, the proof of this influence is everywhere. In 2013, The Boston Beer Company began selling a re-creation of McAuliffe's original New Albion Ale; Sierra Nevada released a collaboration beer between McAuliffe and Grossman called Jack & Ken's Ale as part of its thirtieth anniversary celebration; and even the original signage from New Albion Brewing Company is on display at the Russian River Brewing Company in Santa Rosa, California. The Hopland Brewery, California's first brewpub, was founded in 1983 when owners Michael Laybourn and Norman Franks, homebrewers both, purchased New Albion's old brewing equipment.

"The revival of American beer of the past 30 years is a phenomenon attributable to one of the first (if not the first) 'open-source' collaborative experiences in modern history," Papazian writes on the Brewers Association website. "The community of homebrewers, beer enthusiasts and craft brewers made the pioneers of the democratization of process. It is only anecdotal knowing that Steve Jobs was a member of the 'Homebrew Computer Club,' from which the seeds of the Mac Computer would emerge. The fact is, homebrewers were already fashioning their own revolution before a communication technology emerged that would later enhance the means by which revolutionary ideas and the process of democratizing innovation would be accelerated. Are homebrewers and beer enthusiasts the true heroes of this and tomorrow's day and age?"

CHAPTER 4
COMMUNITY

"As a craft brewer in America, after 27 years we've finally gotten to 1 percent market share, so my competition is not craft brewers because we're all going to succeed or fail together. My real competition is ignorance and apathy. I'm about creating an appreciation of good beer, educating people about it, and teaching them to treat it with respect. If I can do those things, I can succeed."

—Jim Koch, founder, The Boston Beer Company

The first thing to make clear is that these nanobrewers aren't really being paid. They aren't drawing a salary. And they aren't relying on volunteers to keep the lights on, either. They're paying two part-time bar servers, both of whom also have "real" jobs, and are doing everything else—brewing, kegging, cleaning, accounting, maintenance, decorating, etc.—largely on their own. Effectively for free. Revenue growth is steady, and they're turning a modest profit on paper, albeit with only a few paid employees.

And they couldn't be happier about it.

That was the staffing situation at Grandma's House when I first met the owners in 2014, and that was nearly six months into its existence as a bona fide commercial brewing business. The owner, Matthew Fuerst, wasn't getting paid; neither was the manager-slash-bartender for the front of house, his brother Ben, who moved out to Colorado from Ohio just to help get the operation off the ground.

It was as "startup" as a brewery operation gets.

"Our mom wanted Matt to do this back in Cleveland," Ben told me one afternoon over pints at Grandma's House's kitschy, knickknack-filled tasting room on Denver's south side. "It's cheaper there, less competition, but here it seems like everyone who opens does well. For the second location, we might do Cleveland."

They're doing it their own way, that's for sure. Starting with the name: Grandma's House? For a brewery? And carrying over to the whole theme of the place, Grandma's House is easily one of the most unique spaces I've ever gone to drink beer. Located on an up-and-coming stretch of South Broadway near downtown Denver and built into a space that used to house an antique store, the wood-paneled taproom is cool in the exact opposite way that so many sleek, modern taprooms are. Yes, there are farmhouse-style tables and chairs scattered throughout the place. Yes, the bar top itself is fashioned to look like a handmade quilt that's been frozen into place with varnish. Yes, an operational 8-track player is part of the sound system. Yes, the glasses are mismatched thrift store finds, as are the dozens of figurines, vases, prints, and assorted tchotchkes that cover just about every inch of available wall and shelf space. Crochet sleeves cover each tap handle, identifying the available pours, and a retro tube TV and Nintendo game system anchor the center of the room, set up for Fuerst's other passion—hosting events for the local Tetris League.

A velvet Elvis painting hangs on the wall. The brewery's social media account handles are featured in small wooden frames behind the bar, each knit in colorful crochet. The menu is handwritten each day on a blackboard.

It's a different kind of place.

The neighborhood is a somewhat surprising place to find a brewing operation like this one, too. The building is right in the middle of what's known as Denver's Green Mile, one of the busiest stretches of marijuana dispensaries and related businesses in the city. But the white-painted storefront with its greenery-laced awning is hard to miss in all of this. And that's part of the point for Fuerst and Co., being just weird enough to stand out in what is already a crowded market for local brewers.

"Using all of these different glasses is cool, but it makes things a little complicated for the servers," Ben told me one day at the bar as he marked the mismatched glassware with blue dots in strategic spots so the bartenders would know how much to pour in each one. He started by filling a standard pint glass with water to measure the right amount needed for each, and then poured that into his other glasses, including a traditional German-style beer mug, a circa-1980 *Star Wars* collectible glass, and even one shaped like a cowboy boot. The blue dot on the side indicates the proper fill-level regardless of the different shapes and sizes. "If we don't do this, they just fill them all the way up to whatever size it is and we end up way over-serving."

Design details aside, Grandma's House is also very different from most brewing operations in the way its business is set up and the way it operates. Rather than following the standard nano formula—brewing their own recipes, selling their own beers in their tasting room, and maybe distributing locally to nearby restaurants and bars—Grandma's House considers itself a "collaborative brewery," a shared space that effectively functions as an incubator for startup brewers. What that means is that the brewhouse is effectively open to other brewers, often startups themselves, as a place where they can come and brew their recipes on Grandma's House's seven-barrel commercial system, and even sell their beers out front while they're getting their own businesses set up. It's a testing ground, training space, and business accelerator for brewers, all in one.

It also makes for a nice mix of beers on tap in the Grandma's House public space. Early on, one of Matt's recipes, a hatch chile-infused porter, drew raves, but the mix of different brewers with different backgrounds and philosophies and approaches working in the back all but ensures a steady stream of unique flavors in the taproom. I've sampled interesting pilsners there, as well as Belgian-style reds, traditional IPAs, and even a beer brewed using Japanese sake ingredients. As experimental brewing spaces go, the collaborative approach has proven to be an effective way to ensure variety on tap, and that's not something that every brewer—nano or not—can promise in this age of the overcrowded, overhyped craft beer.

At the time that this book was written, Grandma's House had a roster of about six contract brewers working in its space—"grandkids," as they're known—with plans to add more down the road. The idea, Fuerst says, is to graduate out new breweries from the space every six months or so, replacing them with new brewers to keep the collaborative approach of the place rolling.

Community is such an integral part of the craft brewing movement, so identifiable with nanobrewing in particular that it has become one of the defining characteristics of the entire industry. Even the Brewer's Association definition of the prototypical craft brewer—which is an independent brewer that produces less than six million barrels of beer per year and is focused on traditional methods and innovative flavors—acknowledges this side of things, explaining that "craft brewers tend to be very involved in their communities through philanthropy, product donations, volunteerism, and sponsorship of events."

At Grandma's House, this is taken to the next logical step, creating a literal community of brewers, but in general this aspect of the business can be found nationwide among breweries of all shapes and sizes. These businesses are not only about providing quality beers to their communities but also giving back to their neighbors, getting involved with other local businesses, and making sure they're supporting those who live and work around them.

And it all starts with the brewers themselves.

Business is a competitive sport, and commercial brewing is no exception. This is 100 percent a business, no matter how fun or happy-go-lucky it may appear from the outside. These guys are doing this work to make a profit. Not necessarily so they can buy Porsches and retire at thirty, but so they can keep doing the work they enjoy doing without going bankrupt. Profit is a simple fact of life for any small business.

Unlike many other business sectors, brewing is as collegial and community-minded an industry as any I've ever experienced. Yes, there have been lawsuits over beer names and some buyouts and various wranglings over the years, but that is far from the norm, especially at the nano level. In fact, it's not uncommon to see competing owners not only chatting over drinks at each other's establishments but sharing access to equipment, ingredients, knowledge, and even the products themselves via collaboration beers and other one-off projects.

One example of this community aspect in action came to me from Fiction Beer Company, a startup brewery on Denver's east side that opened for business in late 2014. When the owners were installing their mash tun, they realized they had no way to measure the liquid they were adding to the vessel every time they brewed a batch. As a result, they couldn't just turn on the hose and walk away; rather, they had to fill a five-gallon bucket over and over, tipping it into the kettle by hand every time to make sure they added just the right amount of water to their recipes. Nearby craft brewery Station 26 Brewing Company, effectively a competitor, helped the Fiction team solve this problem by lending them a tool that measured the amount of water in their tank at any given time. Valued at more than $1,200—an expense that was not in Fiction's budget in those early days—the tool allowed them to calibrate their equipment and mark where on the tank the water level needed to be, depending on the style they were working on. Not only did the gesture of goodwill save Fiction's founders a significant up-front expense, but it also helped them streamline their brewing process to save both time and money going forward. Station 26, for its part, got karma points and a stronger local competitor in the bargain.

The examples of this sort of thing go on and on. Another good one: Long-mont, Colorado–based Oskar Blues, one of the largest and most successful craft brewers in the state, is known to regularly help nearby startup brewers source ingredients for their beers, adding their orders to its own enterprise-scale hop and malt orders, thereby allowing the tiny upstarts to enjoy the same bulk pricing power that a national producer like Oskar Blues does.

Admittedly, this help-me-and-I'll-help-you approach to business makes sense when you think about the market that craft brewers—and startup nano-brewers in particular—operate in. As of 2014, craft beer made up just a tiny fraction of the total US beer market, so this is still a massive underdog story. The competition for small-time brewers isn't other small-time brewers; it's the multinational conglomerates dominating the market to this day. In this situation, it's in everyone's interest to promote enjoyment of craft beer over the mass-market alternatives, and that often means helping keep the brewery down the road in business by any means necessary, even if it's your direct competitor.

"Craft's fundamental value proposition is that beer lovers are willing to pay a little bit more for a beer that has something more: more flavor, more variety, more local appeal," writes Bart Watson, chief economist with the

Brewers Association. "For the past year, I've been stating the primary reasons for craft beer demand as some combination of the following: fuller-flavor, a variety of flavors/styles, and support for local/independent businesses. Typically, I cite studies that suggest the flavor/variety dimension as the primary driver, with local taking an important, albeit secondary role. But there is increasing evidence that local may be rivaling flavor as a motivating factor for craft beer buyers."

And the numbers back up this trend. According to research conducted by Nielsen and released in early 2015, beer buyers identify "local" as the most important factor driving their beer purchases, peaking at 53 percent of buyers aged 21 to 34. For all beer consumers over 21, that figure is 45 percent.

For nanobrewers, cultivating a community atmosphere—around their taprooms, their employees, and their customers—simply serves to reinforce this aspect of their value proposition. Small-time brewers are, by their very nature, local businesses. Reaching out with philanthropic efforts, organizing fun runs, employing local workers, and all the rest places them firmly as part of the communities they serve, reminding everyone of this and making them the de facto local choice.

"While I think flavor and variety are important and will always provide value added to craft brewer brands, I think it's worth pausing a moment and appreciating how important this sea change is," wrote Watson. "When looking at the longue durée of the beer industry, the hundred years from the 1870s to the 1970s were the opposite of this. They were a century of scale beating small-town production, national marketing campaigns trumping local word of mouth, and a slow shift away from beer markets organized by the distance you could ship fresh beer in a horse drawn cart to ones organized around national networks, refrigerated railcars, industrial efficiency, and national brands. It's taken a lot of hard work on the part of determined small brewers, but local beer is back, and based on the numbers, it's here to stay."

"Basically it's an incubator for people with commercial aspirations," says Preston Hartman with Two Creeks Brewing, one of the first contract brewers to work out of the Grandma's House workspace. "You could just be a homebrewer who wants to be able to have some buddies over and be able to say that you have something on tap; that's fine, and I think he'll always have a few guys like that. But really the idea is you can go there and build your brand and learn how to brew commercially without having to actually get your own building, your own equipment, from day one."

That's essentially what Hartman himself was trying to do when I met with him in late 2014. He was in what he called the "location stage" for his business, looking for an affordable space for his soon-to-be brewhouse and taproom while he maintained his full-time job as a way to pay the bills. In the meantime, however, he was working on the brewing system at Grandma's House in an effort to get his recipes dialed in and build up a local following for his products. He was even able to distribute the beers he brewed, hosting beer-pairing dinners and reaching out to local restaurants and bars before even investing in a brewing system of his own.

Like many new brewers, Hartman got his start brewing up batches in his kitchen. In his case, however, it was wine not beer that got him into the practice. Living in Virginia, he was making fruit wines in flavors that he couldn't find commercially—like pear wine, peach wine, pineapple wine, and banana wine—when he realized that he had a knack for it and really enjoyed the process. Wine production led to beer when he moved to Colorado in 2008, and as Hartman tells it, he decided that, if he was going to dedicate all of his nights and weekends to this hobby, he'd better get really, really good at it and try to make the best product he could. Like a jazz musician spending hours in the woodshed honing his craft, Hartman focused for years on perfecting his skills by brewing only the traditional styles, rather than all sorts of crazy variations, and focusing on ales, stouts, porters, and the other classics. Only then, he says, did he allow himself to branch out, try tweaking his recipes, and get creative.

All bets are off now, however. In addition to Hartman's favorite German-style brews like Schwarzbier and Vienna lager, Two Creeks has also experimented with herb-infused ales as well as several lower-alcohol session IPAs in varieties ranging from a Belgian-style to an IPA-inspired lager brewed with Hartman's house lager yeast instead of the ale yeast more commonly used in IPAs. A dry-hopped take on his Ben's Folly Belgian ale is described as bold and citrusy, with a flavor profile that highlights both candied oranges and cloves, a result of the Amarillo hops used in the brew as well as the Westmalle and Duvel Belgian yeast strains.

The standards-first approach paid off. As of 2014, Hartman was one of the most successful homebrewers in the region by a wide margin, winning a long list of brewing competitions and amateur medals and developing a reputation for unique, high-quality brews that he hoped would eventually carry over to his commercial operation. Word of mouth is everything in the world of amateur brewing, he says, and early customers can be hard to come by without this sort of community support and backing from his peers.

It should also be noted that the homebrewing community goes both ways. On the Two Creeks Brewing website, Hartman offers full, detailed recipes for each of his creations so his brewing peers can re-create and critique his beers. "As always, just ask and you shall receive," he writes.

"Right now it's perfect. I've got a place where I can have my beer on tap and sell it," he says of Grandma's House. "A place where I can raise the stakes, or take too long to brew something and kind of go through some early struggles without a whole lot of consequences. It's really nice. I just tried to take the hobby as far as it could go, so the next step was, if I'm going to come into this industry from the homebrewer side, is there any way for me to operate in somebody else's brewery as a sort of transition step?"

The contract brewing arrangement like that at Grandma's House was something that fledgling brewers had been wanting to do in Colorado for a long time, and it just worked out that Fuerst came along and figured out the legal side of things in a way that made sense for both the contractors and the brewery itself. (Other similar operations exist where professional brewers will allow amateurs to brew their recipes alongside them on full-sized commercial equipment, eventually making the beers available on tap, but for the most part those businesses serve primarily as outlets for dedicated homebrewers instead of commercial incubators.)

The community Hartman sees at Grandma's House fills a need that goes beyond vanity projects. It matters from a real-world business perspective and, he says, can make a real difference in the career aspirations of the area's startup brewers.

"Say you approach some potential investors or a bank and you say, 'Hey, I'm a homebrewer and I want to start a brewery.' Well that raises a lot of questions in people's minds, especially if they're going to give you money," he says. "Do I really know what I'm doing? Do I really have the skills to make this work? So [the Grandma's House setup] is a really cool bridge to be able to say, you know, 'Hey, I really do know how to use this equipment.' I know how to scale up recipes. I know how to sell to my customers. And I've already built a customer base. I can even say I've had a beer release party and sixty of my customers showed up. So it's just a really cool transition that's really helpful for anybody who's trying to come at this from the homebrewer's side and make it a real business."

The truth is, communities of beer drinkers have been gathering together for generations. In the early days, of course, this happened at taverns, beer gardens, and festivals. Then it was bars, clubs, and ball games. But, no matter the setting, the intent and reality was the same: beer is best enjoyed in a group. Beer is a social drink; it always has been.

This fact goes back to the very earliest days of human civilization, predating even the ancient Romans and Greeks, when beverages like beer and wine were social drinks, ever-present at festivals and other gatherings. To some extent, this was a matter of safety—when enjoying mind-altering substances, it has always been wise to have a buddy around to watch your back in case things go south—but the fun to be had when drinking in a group is well known. It has even helped shape the food-and-beverage world as we know it today. For instance, when German brewers discovered that shade trees grown over their underground lagering cellars—where the Bavarian-style beers they brewed were stored to ferment in cooler temperatures, creating the crisp, clear lager beers the region is known for—helped to keep those underground storage rooms cool, it didn't take long for the first brewer to set up tables and benches in these groves so customers could enjoy their beers in shaded comfort, thereby creating the first beer gardens.

For today's nano and small craft brewers, the social history of beer lends itself to the sense of community discussed earlier in this chapter, but the connection between the brewer and their customers can go both ways. Not only do beer drinkers want to be around other beer lovers when they drink, but they also want to feel that sense of connection to the breweries and craftspeople they patronize. It isn't enough just to drink in their brewer's beer garden anymore; they want to know not only what they're drinking, but also the people behind it and their motivations.

"I think [this attitude] goes to the whole community aspect of it," explains Tristan Chan, the founder of a craft beer blog, PorchDrinking.com, which has been cultivating a community of US beer fans online since 2012. "You want to know why these people decided to start a brewery, because it's not an easy endeavor. You want to know what went into brewing the beer that you're drinking. You want to know how a beer got its name or why they choose to brew a certain style."

It all wraps into the greater theme of a small businessperson being more invested in their community, he says, and being more invested in the people that choose to spend their money with them. To some extent, this is an example of marketing over convenience, of buying the story over buying the cheapest product in the store. These days, craft beer—really, really good craft beer even—is available in stores just about nationwide. All the flavor, all the creativity, and all the quality is available for the taking just about anywhere, anytime, for little more than the price of a six-pack. But neighborhood breweries and nanobreweries require a little more effort. Generally, you have to drive to the brewery, talk to the brewer, and fill up your growler or have a pint at the bar if you want to drink their beers. It's more work, but it's also more personal. Chan, for one, believes this part of the transaction is always worth the effort.

"There are so many people that have so many great stories to tell," he says, "and people want to hear those stories. They want to spend their afternoon at a brewery and talk to the people that make their beer. I think that's one of the most enjoyable aspects of the craft, getting to know the people that are behind the beer."

On the flip side, many neighborhood brewers look to strengthen these connections by hosting benefits for local causes, giving a percentage of their profits back to the community, and other efforts. (This isn't limited exclusively to nanos, of course. Even larger, more established brewers do this, often working with local small businesses and taking other steps to remain invested in their communities.) Still, giving back is something that's more attainable when a brewer's customers spend their money locally rather than just going to the corner liquor store for a craft six-pack. Because they as a business are invested in the community they belong to, their customers' community, they want to see it thrive and succeed, and they're reinvesting back into that community as a result.

Chan says it was this spirit of collaboration, this camaraderie among brewers, that inspired him to start *PorchDrinking* in the first place. It was 2009, and he was working with AmeriCorps, on a bare-bones AmeriCorps living allowance, in Fort Collins, Colorado. Since money was tight, he spent most weekends hanging around the taproom at New Belgium Brewing Company, which was one of the cheaper places in town to drink in those days. In the process, he ended up learning a lot about the craft beer industry from the bartenders there. But one thing stood out to him: if New Belgium ever ran out of a certain kind of hops, or a certain kind of malt, they could (and did) just go down the street to Odell Brewing Company or Fort Collins Brewery or another nearby craft brewer and simply "borrow" some for the day, with the understanding that they would soon enough be able to return the favor when someone else was running low. The fact that they were working so closely with their competitors, and the collaborative nature of the industry in general, floored him. It was unlike anything he had ever seen in business before—the fact that brewers of all types can coexist in one place while celebrating each other's successes.

"Craft beer is definitely starting to feel some growing pains here and there with all the litigation that's happening," he says, "but that in its essence is really about trying to protect their brands and the quality of their products. But at its core, craft beer is about collaboration, and that really ties into the working with local businesses, working with local nonprofits, and really trying to invest in the communities that they belong to. All of those beliefs are wrapped into craft brewing's core values."

The two thousand square feet of open space between the taproom and the Grandma's House brewhouse itself—which used to be filled to the rafters with furniture, lamps, mirrors, and other treasures when it was still an antique store—is today largely filled with Fuerst's leftover flea market finds, a few old computers, and the assorted stock of the previous tenants. The two-story room has a mezzanine, wrapping around on three sides, and soaring ceilings with high windows that let in a surprising amount of light, despite the dark, dusty wood that makes up the interior. Fuerst had previously planned on extending his taproom into this middle space before deciding to keep it small to start, leaving only the front room as the bar space. He has considered opening a brewpub in the space, as he has plenty of room for not only a dining room, but also a kitchen and prep area, but he doesn't want to dilute the work he and the brewers are doing by overextending himself.

"It's still a possibility," he says, "but the only way I would do it is if someone came on and took it over as their thing. I don't want anything to do with it. I'm still learning the brewery side so I don't need the extra learning curve of running a restaurant on top of that."

His real goal in creating a collaborative brewery, he says as we sit at an old oak farmtable in the back room, a relic from the building's antique store days, is to create an environment where like-minded brewers can get together, share knowledge, and learn about the industry today.

"I know enough about brewing to know that there's a lot to learn," he says. "And, while I have the knowledge base, we don't have a professional brewer here. We have a lot of people who know a very decent amount about beer, so we have complementary knowledge bases, and hopefully we can all benefit from that. Hopefully all of our beer gets better as a result of being in this culture."

The fact is, although many of the brewers working at Grandma's House are accomplished homebrewers, none of them had worked on real, professional equipment (including Fuerst himself) until they started brewing at this facility. Naturally, there's a learning curve involved. Given the scale of a seven-barrel brewing system, there is a step up in terms of ingredients, recipes, and brew schedules when moving from the homebrew level, all of which new commercial brewers need to address as they make the transition from hobbyists to professionals. When you're brewing on a five- or ten-gallon system, you're probably not going to do all of the nitpicky things like test pH and run starch tests as you go. But at the commercial scale, it all matters; these are the little things that separate good beer from exceptional beer.

"I just bought a microscope because I want to be better about analyzing our yeast cultures," Fuerst says. "I actually had to dump a batch because I was pushing it with the yeast and we had a contamination issue. I don't know any homebrewers that are putting their yeast under the microscope, but that's a real thing that you should be doing when you're brewing at this level."

As for the collective brewery idea itself, Fuerst says he was motivated not only by the competition he saw in the market and the fact that he needed to differentiate himself, but also by the fact that this sort of incubator space was very much needed in the fast-growing nanobrewing community.

"This is the first cooperative, or collective as I call it, brewery in the state," he says, "and there's only a handful in the country. This kind of idea had popped up in certain areas like Houston, and there's one in Cleveland; areas where the craft beer scene is still sort of early on in its development. But I think it almost makes more sense in an area like this where new breweries are just popping up like weeds, and we're now to the point where it's arguable how many the city can sustain. I felt there's a place both for the consumer who's looking for something new and unique, and the brewers themselves to have an intermediate step where they can brew on a more serious level before sinking in all the money it takes to do this."

It's a high-minded business goal, to be sure, but it's rooted in the hard truths of food service: if a customer comes to your brewery early on and doesn't like your product, they won't come back, especially given all of the new options now available across the country. Never mind that brewing beer is difficult and can be tricky to do well early on; like a chef with a new restaurant, first impressions mean everything. For potential brewery owners, this can be particularly daunting, given the significant up-front expenses involved in building a commercial brewhouse. By the time they've installed all of their equipment, signed a lease on their space, built out their taproom, and hired staff, they may very well be seven figures into their business, and that's before they even get to open the doors and serve to paying customers. With that overhead, it's fairly obvious why a brewer would want to start selling as soon as humanly possible, even if their beer isn't yet up to the level that it eventually will be.

So Grandma's House sits in the middle of these two opposing forces: the need to start selling beer immediately to start bringing in revenue and the need to spend time on a commercial system learning how to brew at scale. As such, it serves as a sort of safe middle ground where brewers can come to test out their new product ideas and generate a little startup capital by selling their beers to customers yet also take the time to learn how to brew on a real, grown-up, full-sized system.

"I hope that this allows them to get their recipes dialed in on a true system," Fuerst says. "Everyone will tell you that just going from one system to another, even if it's the same size, it's going to be different and you'll need to make adjustments. Here the idea is that you can get all that ironed out in [a] safe environment, maybe get some honest feedback from consumers that aren't your buddies, and get your company name out there. It should be beneficial for them, and I'm hoping that it's a win-win for both of us."

For Emily Thomason and Adam Frank, two of Fuerst's earliest contract brewers at Grandma's House, it certainly worked out that way. The married couple was in the midst of planning and launching Broken Spine Brewing, their own entry into the nano market, when I met with them in 2015. The idea itself had been in the works for at least two years at that point, while both still worked at their full-time jobs in the financial services industry. But it really took shape when they gained access to the full-sized equipment at Grandma's House. As experienced homebrewers, they were looking to take their efforts to the next level when they stumbled across Fuerst's operation.

"It's very different," Frank says of brewing on the seven-barrel system at Grandma's House, admitting that he did a lot of research before brewing his first batch at scale. He not only reached out to the other brewers at Grandma's but also brewers at other craft operations in town, in hopes of getting a better idea as to what the differences would really be like. In truth, he says, it comes down to a lot of trial and error, of making mistakes and adapting to them. The idea that a homebrewer can roll up and expect that their existing recipes are going to work as expected on a larger system just isn't the reality of the situation. As a result, it can be hard to judge just how different the process is going to be at the commercial scale, and that can mean different levels of hop utilization, a longer boil until the break, or even changes in yeast behavior. It's just different.

"I don't know if I'll say we're being conservative with the recipes we're doing on the larger system, but kind of we are," Frank says. "We're pulling back on certain things, to play it safe, and that's sort of why we chose a Belgian blonde to start with as our first beer on that system. Something that isn't going to have tons of specialty malts or other different ingredients. It's a little bit, maybe *simple* isn't the right term, but we know the recipe. We know that beer. And I figure if it turns out a little hoppier or bitter than expected that's not necessarily a bad thing."

We were meeting at Alpine Dog Brewing on Denver's east side, sipping on stouts while a late winter snow fell outside. Frank and Thomason are representative of a growing trend in the craft-brewing world: part-time brewers who plan to take their side gig full time in the near future without quitting their day jobs. It's a way, as some see it, to take the homebrewing hobby "professional" without having to commit your livelihood to it. But, as financial planners, the cautious approach makes sense for the Broken Spine cofounders. ("It's scary trying to take that leap," Thomason admits.)

The pair met in Seattle, developing their own love of beer on road trips up and down the West Coast, before moving back to Colorado, where Frank went to college, in 2011. By 2015, they were just starting to make their dream a reality. That's a long time to mull a career change and points to the pair's measured approach to the business. Frank was even participating in a university-backed brewing science program when I met him, complete with an internship, to prepare for the leap.

"Everything you read on the brewing forums, they're always like 'do not go over 7 barrels,'" Frank says of their plan to launch on a 2.5-barrel system. "Some say 7, others say 10. And it's funny, we had this guy who brewed for Alaskan in class who went through this whole thing where he said he would never open a place smaller than 15 barrels. But then he was like, 'You've got to understand, I'm older, I just don't have the energy. I've brewed on big systems. I know what the difference is. If you love it, everything I just said gets thrown out the window. You can work your way up that way.' There is a lot less to invest in when everything is that much smaller."

Career switching in the brewing industry is fairly common. It's a high-growth industry, in a popular segment of the food and beverage business, so many professionals from other industries are making the move. It's even more common among those who are already tangentially associated with the industry. For example, Thomason and Frank met their attorney in Seattle when they were just getting started on the Broken Spine project. A few years later, he moved to Asheville, North Carolina, and started a brewery of his own, augmenting his beer-focused law practice with his brewing proceeds. And it happened again when they moved to Denver, where their insurance agent is also one of the owners of Goldspot Brewing Company, a new independent brewery on the city's north side.

Is it just a factor of environment? One of those things that, once people get involved and start doing every day, they want to find out what brewing is like themselves? Frank says yes, explaining that the friendly nature of the industry, compared to what most people do for a living, plays into it.

"One thing I love about brewing is it's so diverse," he says. "It's one of those industries where you really get people from all over. You have your engineer types who are really good at getting things exact. And then you have more artistic breweries. It's just kind of all over the board."

And that extends to the clientele as well, Thomason says. You're just as likely to sit down at a taproom next to a hipster beer geek as you are someone's grandfather or a young family of four. Babies are not uncommon in breweries. The industry is one that draws a lot of different types of people together.

"It's just cool that you get that," Frank says. "And, kind of like music or art, everyone has a different taste. So maybe you don't like this beer, maybe it's not to your taste, but there are so many options out there now that you can almost pinpoint what you do and don't like. Maybe it's the kind of hops, maybe it's the style. Whatever it is, it's not a bad beer, it just isn't to your taste."

CHAPTER 5
STYLES

"We're the best thing that's happened to this industry since the repeal of prohibition. And, at the same time, we need to be absolutely vigilant about how our beers look, smell, and taste when they get to our customers' lips."

—Kim Jordan, cofounder, New Belgium Brewing Company, speaking at the 2013 Craft Brewers Conference

What makes US craft beer different from the lagers and ales the rest of the world drinks? The recipes and the diversity of styles that we brew in this country. One of the things that makes American brewing unique, in fact, is that brewers here try to re-create styles from all over the world, rather than focusing on any one "American" style. They import German malts to brew German-style lagers; they find real Belgian yeast strains to add that fruity, funky Brett kick to their farmhouse ales and saisons; and they source hops from all over to flavor their beers in all sorts of different and unique ways. In this way, American brewers are some of the most international on the planet, adapting the best beer styles from all over the world and putting their own personal spin on them, brewing them with the ingredients, equipment, and flavors we have access to in this country.

International brewers, for the most part, don't do this. They brew what they brew—and they do it very well, mind you—but they generally don't try to be everything to everyone. German brewers brew German beers, for example. And, although it's difficult to point to any one craft style as "American," there is something very US-centric about brewing many different kinds of beers to appeal to many different kinds of beer lovers.

But the country-by-country nature of most brewing is primarily due to the regional nature of yeast strains—Belgian yeasts are typically found in Belgium, German yeasts in Germany, etc.—that traditionally limited the number of different beer styles a brewer could make at any given time. To this day, the tradition of "house beers" remains strong in Europe, where stylistic selection is limited and the specialty of the house is generally the beer you'd want to order anyway.

In the United States, of course, things are different. Here, it's not uncommon to find ten to twelve different styles on a brewery's beer list—it's almost disappointing not to—and as such the focus is more on addressing each of the major styles rather than creating specialties. It's about the brewer putting their own personal spin on each style, offering their interpretation, rather than specializing in any one. Feel like a brown ale? You're covered. A light lager? No problem. An oak-aged pale ale? Done. (The Alchemist brewery in Waterbury, Vermont, is one of the notable exceptions to this unwritten rule of US brewing, crafting just one beer—its American double IPA, Heady Topper—which has for many years been widely considered among the best US-made beers. Although the brewery itself no longer serves directly to the public, as of 2015 The Alchemist produces 180 barrels of its flagship IPA per week in twelve 15-barrel batches. No more, no less.) True, many brewers do specialize in particular styles: New Belgium Brewing in Fort Collins, Colorado, will probably always be known first and foremost as the creator of Fat Tire Amber Ale, the caramel- and biscuit-flavored beer the company has been producing since the early 1990s, but variety often wins out when it's time to plan a tasting-room menu.

Speaking of IPAs, US craft brewers have long been associated with the big, bitter IPAs that they produce, but, in truth, US brewing has moved beyond the hop monsters in recent years to embrace beer variety in all its forms. And it's a long list: lagers, pilsners, pale ales, wheat beers, brown ales, porters, stouts, saisons, sours, and more. The various styles run the gamut from dry and crisp (lagers), to malt heavy and rich (porters and stouts), to hoppy and high alcohol (IPAs and barleywines).

"There is a lot more to a style than just whether it's light or dark," writes John Palmer in *How to Brew*. "Each beer style has a characteristic taste, imparted by either the yeast, the malts, the hops, the water, or all four. A style is best defined by naming all the ingredients and the fermentation particulars. Change any one item, and you have probably hopped into another style category."

For nanobrewers, this fact works to their advantage. Uniqueness and variety are a big part of the appeal of visiting a small, neighborhood brewery, where naming all the ingredients and explaining the fermentation particulars for every beer on the menu is all but expected. These operations cater to a savvy clientele that wants to know exactly what's going on in their beer. Doughnut infused ale? MillerCoors could never do that given its scale, but Fiction Brewing sure can. Chai tea stout? That probably wouldn't fly off the shelves at a Major League Baseball game the same way Bud Light does, but an audience for it is there (and it's delicious, by the way). It's all about creating flavors that customers can't find anywhere else and keeping them on their toes with new presentations, styles, and combinations. Like a chef working a seasonal menu that highlights what's fresh, variety is a big part of what makes neighborhood brewing a unique businesses model and it's one of the things that, by keeping customers on their toes, ensures that they come back again and again.

"So we like to keep it dark in the brewhouse; makes it seem more mysterious," Fiction Brewing Company co-owner Ryan Kilpatrick tells me as we make our way through the darkened tanks next to his taproom one Friday night. Kilpatrick, who started Fiction—a literature-themed brewery that also hosts live bluegrass bands and trivia nights—with his wife, Christa, in 2014, was still working full time as an accountant when we met, so he tends to brew in the evenings when he's better able to find free time. Friday nights are a favorite for him, since not only can he work until the wee hours without worrying about getting to the office the next day, but the crowd at the bar seems to enjoy watching the process unfold as they sip on the final product nearby.

"Gotta brew in the dark," laughs assistant brewer Chris Marchio as he moves hoses that will eventually be used for the sparge into place on the brewhouse floor. "Talk about a first-world problem."

Fiction, located along a somewhat forgotten stretch of Colfax Avenue just east of downtown Denver, brews on a seven-barrel system, providing more than enough capacity for its taproom sales as well as limited distribution. Like many nanobrewers, Kilpatrick got his start in the business as a dedicated homebrewer, trying (and failing, he says) at various beer recipes for years before perfecting his process and, eventually, setting his sights on moving into commercial production. This background is clear when considering the beers he keeps on tap at Fiction—including everything from an experimental green tea chocolate milk stout, to a rhubarb black current wheat, a German gose, a Belgian dark strong ale with roasted Hatch green chile, and an experimental Pilsner with fruity American hops—as well as his penchant to take sometimes ridiculous chances when tinkering with flavors. For example, shortly after Fiction opened, he brewed a doughnut-infused bourbon barrel porter in collaboration with local doughnut shop Glazed and Confuzed that included actual doughnuts in the mix.

And he likes it this way, calling the work he does at Fiction "commercial homebrewing." He enjoys the experimentation and freedom that comes with owning his place, as well as the flexibility that his customer base offers. They expect him to take chances with flavors and styles; they aren't coming to Fiction for lagers and standard ales, and that frees him up to get creative with beer styles.

"We've brewed with plums, we've brewed with chocolate, we've brewed with star anise, we've brewed with the fruit of the cascara tree," he says in the darkened brewhouse. "That last one was tough. It was for a collaboration beer and we couldn't find it anywhere. I ended up going to a local coffee shop, Corvus Coffee, who happened to have a few hundred extra pounds lying around. We got the chocolate—forty pounds of it—on Amazon."

While we talk, he walks over to Chris, who's watching the brew vessel as it comes up to temperature. "How does that boil look? The color and texture. How fast is it?"

At one point, Fiction worked on a collaboration brew that called for them to include a plant called sea buckthorn in the recipe. A quick Wikipedia check confirmed that sea buckthorn, also known as hippophae, is a shrub that is native to most of Europe and parts of central Asia. Its fruit—a small, yellow-orange berry harvested by being frozen off the branch before being crushed and frozen in bulk—is high in Vitamin C and is noticeably sour in its raw state, more like a cranberry than an orange. But once sweetened with a little sugar, the fruit offers a nice, clean flavor that doesn't overwhelm the other flavors it is paired with. Known as the Siberian pineapple, sea buckthorn is often compared to sour apple and sour orange flavors with a bit of a berry aftertaste.

Interesting for a beer, for sure, but how do you get it in the United States, where it's not grown and not widely used? As with most things at Fiction, Kilpatrick eventually found the fruit he needed via an online supplier, but it didn't come cheap. "It's the strange ingredients that are always the most expensive," he says. "Malt, hops, yeast . . . we can get all of that around here. But when you want to do something different, it can add up."

In the brewhouse, the temperature keeps rising as the kettle reaches 200 degrees, then 201, then 204. Once the brew hits the protein break, also sometimes called the hot break—meaning the point in the boil when the protein-heavy foam that has formed on the top of the liquid starts to gather and fall back into the wort—Marchio starts watching the clock; the hop and flavoring additions are set to begin shortly after the break.

At Fiction, this is done with a series of numbered plastic buckets. Like a home chef with their ingredient bowls, each bucket is measured and prepared ahead of time, set to be added depending on the schedule Marchio monitors via the Brewers' Dashboard brewery control system software on his laptop. Kilpatrick's brewhouse is fully wired with temperature sensors on each of the brew kettles as well as liquid level sensors and remote controllers for each step in the process—he could brew from his house over the Internet if he really wanted to, he tells me, or at least keep track of the process as it happens in real time. But the software also serves as a virtual checklist for the brewer so that each step happens, per the recipe, at the right time and in the right order. Marchio checks the laptop constantly, well aware that one mistimed step or one missed addition could mean the difference between a good beer and a blown batch.

The night I spent brewing with them, Kilpatrick and Marchio were working on a recipe of Chris's own design, a sauvignon blanc–infused ale with kiwis for sweetness. ("Do kiwis throw off fermentation?" Kilpatrick asked at one point, questioning whether they would need to account for the acid levels in the fruit and adjust the schedule. They never did find out for sure.) The wine grapes were straightforward—sixteen liters worth of home winemaking kits—but sickly sweet in concentrated form. It was a tan, sugary goo that went directly into the wort before the hops, which were from New Zealand themselves, keeping with the overall kiwi theme of the beer. Sugars in beer help make for a dry finish, Marchio explained, since the yeast will convert it all to alcohol as part of the fermentation process. Brewers usually accomplish this by adding granulated sugar to the mix before fermenting, but with this recipe, the sweet grapes served part of this purpose alongside the sugar.

"I want it to taste like gooseberries, white wine, all of the above," Marchio grins.

"When you're brewing with fruit like kiwis, you have to add it slowly because you want them to ferment but you don't want to lose that sweetness," Kilpatrick explains as we wait. "So you dump some, let it ferment, dump some more and let that ferment. Then you 'crash' it and dump the rest for the sake of sweetness and move it to the cold room to condition for three weeks."

The taproom at Baere Brewing Company in Denver—wood paneled, sleek, and modern as it is—somewhat belies the 1970s-era strip mall where it is located, just off a major north-south artery near downtown. In reality, this is the kind of place you could easily miss driving by if you weren't looking for it, and easily discount as a waste of time if you did see it. Next door is a tax services office; down the way, a laundromat. The car wash across the street certainly attracts more traffic, especially in the summers. Baere is even difficult to actually get to when you're really trying—not only is parking a challenge in the neighborhood, but Baere itself is only open a few days per week, in part to accommodate the staff's full-time jobs and in part because they only have so much beer available on a weekly basis and don't want to run out.

But cofounders Ryan Skeels and Kevin Greer, who run the operation on a small, two-and-a-half-barrel brewing system, like it this way. They like flying under the radar a little bit, being a little mysterious and hard to get to. This way, they're a destination, a prize for true connoisseurs to discover.

It's a true labor of love. As of this writing, Greer was still working full-time as an engineer, and Skeels was in the wastewater treatment field—both career paths that allow them the free time they need to brew, they say.

"When we first opened it was just on Thursdays and Saturdays because we didn't want to run out of beer," Greer laughs, "so we didn't want to punch into Friday and risk that. But we never have run out. We've had nine beers on tap consistently with the exception of a handful of times."

Skeels agrees. Having multiple beers on tap can be challenging for breweries of their size, especially when first starting out and trying to determine what kind of demand they'll see. Stocking the bar with the interesting, creative beers they wanted to make at Baere, let alone good beers that people actually wanted to drink and pay for, just increases the challenge. Their big thing at the time, he says, was they wanted to make sure that when people walked in the door, they had at least one option on the board that they would like.

"There's always a primary," he says. "So when you come back a month later, it's the same options or at least something you know you like that you can order."

That's not to say they don't brew some pretty far-out styles, though. Baere's top seller, which happened to be what all three of us were enjoying as we talked in the taproom, is the Big Hoppy Brown, a traditional brown ale that's been kicked up with a mixture of grains including pale, chocolate, and crystal malts along with red wheat, Northern Brewer, and Cascade hops. Unlike most browns, which tend toward the mellower, sweeter side, this one packs a bitter, hoppy punch that tastes more like a dark pale ale than a more typical brown. And that's just the beginning. The taproom—and remember, this is a part-time endeavor for both founders and most of the staff—is usually stocked with at least ten beers of various styles and flavors, often including a wit, a saison, their Baere-liner weisse, an Irish red, their imperial IPA, a farmhouse-style ale and even a locally made Kombucha, a type of lightly fermented tea that's made somewhat like beer and offers some similar flavor notes, without the alcohol.

When the planning for Baere started, the cofounders say they went in with the attitude that they would brew Belgian- and American-style ales, and that would be it. But reality stepped in to complicate things. The brewhouse in their facility only has enough space for three fermenters, and the founders realized very quickly that their building came with some unique tempera-ture-control quirks (having neighbors on both sides, including a laundromat, can make it difficult to maintain a set temperature, and the strip mall layout offers minimal insulating space behind the brewhouse wall, which doesn't help). Fortunately, the realities of their space turned out to be well suited to the brewing of Belgian beers, which are some of their favorites to both make and drink.

"We love saisons," they say. "We love the freedom the style intends. We love low mash temperatures and high fermentation temperatures. Saison means season and this is just what our saisons bring, a variety of palate quenchers for you to enjoy."

Still, as Baere has grown up, it has had to face some of the more unpleas-ant realities of the business world, like theft. Kegs have been stolen, they have found parts of their taproom on Craigslist, and the list goes on and on. It had already been happening when I met them, in fact. Shortly after the brewery opened, Greer found a set of Baere taster glasses for sale on eBay, apparently swiped from the tasting room by an early customer. The seller is at least con-sistent, though, as he was also offering glassware and souvenirs from fellow Denver area nano and neighborhood craft brewers like Former Future Brewing Company, Our Mutual Friend Brewing Company, Jagged Mountain Brewery, and nearly half a dozen others. There is clearly a market for this stuff.

"We get emails a lot from people in places like Poland, Sweden, the Czech Republic and all that," Skeels says, "just asking us to send them coasters or stickers. It's always kind of a different story, but basically, in broken English, it's them saying that they would really like to have some of our stuff up on the wall, like, 'I'm building out my beer cave.' So maybe some of these people are actual collectors and are buying this stuff off eBay, but as much as I love Stone Brewing Company, I wouldn't go online and buy a taster for five bucks."

Still, the upsides of owning a nanobrewery of their size do tend to outweigh the negatives, they admit.

"I don't brew very often anymore," Skeels says, "but I do always try to remember that I get to go to work every day and brew beer. I don't have to do that, but I get to. And I try to remember that every day. [In this neighborhood] we get a lot of people sleeping out front and going through the garbage and stuff like that, so it's important to remember that, no matter how tough the business is, things could be much worse than they are now. That's always a pretty good reminder of what matters."

Greer agrees: "And we have great feedback here. Being on a small system, I think while we do some of the same beers regularly, there's a lot of experimentation that we get to do, and that's a lot of fun."

For generations following Prohibition, beer in the United States meant light lagers, for reasons discussed in an earlier chapter. In the 1980s, however, that began to change, and the rise of craft beer has only accelerated since then.

The craft brewing movement has expanded our palates over the last twenty-plus years, not only by brewing more flavorful styles, but also by introducing lesser-known varieties, like saisons, barleywines, and farmhouse ales to American palates. And that's to say nothing of the experimentation that's gone on, with new ingredients, techniques, and combinations bringing all sorts of new flavors to the table. The options are nearly limitless, and they're still growing every year.

In fact, the Great American Beer Festival (GABF), organized by the Brewers Association and held every September in Denver, judges entries in ninety-two different, officially sanctioned categories, many with several different subcategories of their own. For instance, the American Style Wheat Beer category includes judging for both Light American Wheat Beers without Yeast and Dark American Wheat Beers without Yeast. And, like a dog show, each style category comes with its own lists of ideal characteristics and "best of breed" attributes that brewers are shooting for. Light American Wheat Beers, for example, should be "straw to light amber [in color]," according to the GABF standard. "Low fruity-ester aroma is typical, as is low to medium-low malt aroma. No yeast aroma should be present." The standard even dictates how much of an alcohol smell the beer should give off (none, in this case), what the body of drink should look like (very low to medium), what the original gravity versus final gravity ratio should be, and how bitter the beer can be (10 to 35 IBUs for Light American Wheats).

That's very specific and very strict to the style, but that's the point of a judged competition like the GABF—to not only find the best of the best in terms of product quality, but also to define the standards of each style category for the industry.

BeerAdvocate magazine takes a more casual approach to beer styles, writing: "Simply put, a beer style is a label given to a beer that describes its overall character and often times its origin. It's a name badge that has been achieved over many centuries of brewing, trial and error, marketing, and consumer acceptance." (That said, the publication's list includes 105 individual styles, compared to the 92 officially recognized by the GABF.)

Most craft brewers, of course, aren't brewing all these different styles themselves. They're picking and choosing their favorites and leaving others to tackle the rest. As a general rule, about a dozen different styles appear on most independent brewery tap lists at any time, including:

Pale Ale: The GABF judges pale ales in six different categories, making them one of the most diverse beer styles on the planet and a mainstay at craft brewery taprooms. Based on pale malts, hence the name, copper-colored pale ales carry moderate hop aromas, stronger malt flavors, and medium bitterness that allow the fruity-ester flavors of the hops to shine through. Officially, the pale ale category includes the classic English-style pale ale, Australian-style pale, an "international-style," and the Belgian-style pale. American-style pale ales are punched-up versions of their international cousins, in terms of flavor and, often, alcohol content. According to the GABF guidelines, "the 'traditional' style of this beer has its origins with certain floral, fruity, citrus-like, piney, resinous, or sulfur-like American hop varietals. One or more of these hop characters is the perceived end, but the perceived hop characters may be a result of the skillful use of hops of other national origins." The category also includes the American-style strong pale ale, which brings stronger hop aromas, slightly more malt flavors and, of course, more alcohol (up to 7 percent) to the style.

India Pale Ale: So named for the English-made ales prepared for export to British East India Company employees and other expats in India and the South Pacific in the nineteenth century (the first use of the term *India Pale Ale* is said to be an advertisement in the Australian newspaper, *Sydney Gazette and New South Wales Advertiser*, in 1829), India Pale Ales (IPAs) are today known for their hoppy, bitter flavors and often high alcohol content. A subset of the pale ale category, the standard English IPA is defined by the GABF as a crisp, dry beer with medium to strong hop aroma and flavor, with the end goal being the showcase of the "earthy and herbal English-variety hop character." American-style beers of this type, on the other hand, are often stronger in flavor and alcohol content, with a (sometimes intense) citrus or pine aroma, depending on the type of hops used in the recipe, and tend toward bitterness over balance. Whereas English IPAs can range from 35 to 63 IBUs, American IPAs go from 50 to 70, resulting in a much more bitter flavor.

Imperials: The Imperial variety of any style kicks everything up another notch. Imperial IPAs, for example, show "very high" hop characteristics, strong alcohol content (from 7.6 percent to 10.6 percent) and bitterness that is very high but not harsh. "The intention of this style of beer is to exhibit the fresh and evident character of hops." Well-known commercial Imperial IPAs include Pliny the Elder from Russian River Brewing Company, Heady Topper from The Alchemist, and Dogfish Head Brewery's 90 Minute IPA.

Imperial-style stouts, porters, and other varieties are also common and are made with double or triple the amount of malt and hops as compared to typical batches of each style, resulting in extremely flavorful, alcohol-rich (12 percent imperials are not unheard of) beers. Use of the term *Imperials* to describe these big beers dates back to the nineteenth century, when English brewers made beer specifically for export to the Russian royal family, though the term has evolved throughout the years to more generally describe the biggest, baddest beers a specific brewer makes.

Stout: It's easy to lump all stouts together as Guinness-like beers and be done with it, but in reality the category is quite varied, accounting for nine different varieties at the Great American Beer Fest. True, the standard for stout—the Classic Irish-Style Dry Stout—is most closely identified with Guinness Extra Stout (which is understandable, since the centuries-old brand is currently sold in more than 120 countries with sales reaching more than 220 million gallons per year), and its thick, rich head and coffee-like flavors, but there is more to stout than the Irish classic. The style is largely defined by the use of roasted barley, hence the dark color of the final beer, and brings with it rich, malty overtones. These are not hoppy beers (although the American-style stout is identified by its somewhat higher hop character, it is not a bitter beer). Rather, they are predominantly focused on the mild flavor of the underlying malt, with any bitterness only serving to balance the natural sweetness of the style. Stouts are also not low-alcohol beers by definition. True, Guinness Original/Extra Stout and the brand's Draught offerings all top out at 4.3 percent ABV, while many other stouts range up to 9 percent, with Imperial varieties reaching as high as 12 percent.

Brown Ale: A darker version of a pale ale due to the darker-colored malts used in the brew, both English-style brown ales and American-style brown ales offer a roasted malt character, caramel and biscuit flavors, and low hop bitterness in an easy-drinking, mild beer style. According to the GABF, the American-style brown ales favored by most US craft breweries are slightly hoppier than their European cousins (Delaware-based Dogfish Head Brewery brews what it calls an India Brown Ale, which is dry-hopped like an IPA for strong hop bitterness in what is otherwise a malt-forward brown ale. As mentioned previously, Baere offers a similar twist on this style, as well) but the focus of the style remains on the roasted malt flavor and the slightly sweet characteristics it offers.

Wheat Ale: Wheat beers are, according to the GABF guidelines, an "Americanized version" of the traditional German hefeweizen, brewed with a higher concentration of wheat than barley malt, which gives them a dry but fruity flavor without much hop bitterness. They are usually pale to golden in color, with a hazy, unfiltered appearance, light to medium body, and high carbonation. In the United States, these easy-drinking beers are often enjoyed in the hot summer months and served with a slice of lemon or orange on the glass to play up the fruit flavors of the style. A mainstay of the craft brewing community, some of the better-known American wheat beers include Goose Island's 312 Urban Wheat, Wailua Wheat from Kona Brewing Company, and Solace from Firestone Walker Brewing Company.

Lager: Lager style beers are fundamentally different from ales, not in terms of their ingredients but in the way they are brewed. *BeerAdvocate* defines lagers as beers that are "brewed with bottom-fermenting yeast that work slowly at around 34 degrees Fahrenheit, and are often further stored at cool temperature to mature. Lager yeast produce fewer by-product characters than ale yeast which allows for other flavors to pull through, such as hops." One of the world's oldest, most fundamental styles of beer, lagers are particularly associated with German brewing—the word *lager* itself is derivative of the German word *lagern,* meaning "to store," as in at cold temperatures during the fermentation process.

Lager remains a major category in craft brewing as well: the GABF judges twenty-four different lager beer styles, including different categories for American, German, and other European varieties. Overall, the style is noted for its light golden color, rich head, and bright, hoppy flavor, though US brewers have recently begun playing with this standard recipe, creating black lagers, rye lagers, and more. Popular varieties of the traditional style, particularly in Germany, include Pilsner, Bock, Dunkel, and Schwarzbier. The California Common, also known as Steam Beer when speaking specifically of the beer made by Anchor Brewing in San Francisco, is an American-style beer that is brewed with a unique type of lager yeast that can survive at warmer temperatures, allowing brewers to ferment their beers faster without cooling. This was important in nineteenth-century California, where refrigeration was hard to come by, effectively creating a new type of beer in the process of solving a production problem.

It is worth noting, however, that although still very popular, lager styles have been hurt in the eyes of some by the work of large commercial brewers throughout the years, particularly the American macrobrewing operations and their light-bodied, pale beers. As described by *BeerAdvocate,* many of these beers feature "low bitterness, thin malts, and moderate alcohol." The focus, they write, of these American lagers is "less on flavor and more on mass-production and consumption, cutting flavor and sometimes costs with adjunct cereal grains, like rice and corn." And the list of beers of this particular sort is long and includes everything from Budweiser from Anheuser-Busch, to Miller Genuine Draft, Pabst Blue Ribbon, Corona Extra, and Coors Banquet among many, many others.

Scotch Ale: A subset of the ale category, Scotch ales are broken down further by the GABF into Traditional Scotch Ale and Peated Scotch Ale, differentiated primarily by the amount of smoky peat flavor present in the beer. Either way, Scottish ales are generally identified by their deep copper color and rich, malty flavor, the result of an extended boil during the brewing process that actually caramelizes the wort slightly in the kettle. Scotch ales are also very lightly hopped, resulting in an almost sweet flavor that highlights the malt content of the beer over all else. Like Scotch whiskeys, some brewers like to age their Scotch ales on peat to impart a deep, smoky background flavor, though not all Scotches feature this.

One of the better known Scotch ales on the market, Odell Brewing Company's flagship beer, 90 Shilling, highlights another aspect of Scottish brewing: namely, the country's historical method for pricing beer. In the nineteenth century, Scottish authorities taxed brews by the shilling based on quality or strength, resulting in shilling-based names for various styles of beer that were based on these factors—60 shillings for Light beers (under 3.5 percent ABV), 70 shillings for Heavy beers between 3.5 and 4.0 percent ABV, 80 shillings for Export beers between 4.0 percent and 5.5 percent ABV, and 90 shillings for Wee Heavy beers, or those over 6.0 percent ABV. In fact, Odell's 90 Shilling is actually a lighter take on the traditional Scotch ale style that brings the style's smooth mouthfeel to what is a more medium-bodied amber ale. It doesn't add up to the traditional shilling name, however, with only 5.3 percent ABV.

Red Ale: Red ales generally fill in the space between pale ales and dark ales, meaning the style itself is distinctive primarily in terms of what it is not more than what it is. That said, most red ales are malt-forward and medium on the hop bitterness, tending toward light fruit flavors and toasted malts, with darker malts used during the brewing process to bring out the signature color. This shows up in competition—as many as four different "reds" are judged, in four entirely different style categories: an Irish-style red (which is roughly the standard for what most people associate with reds, thanks to Killian's Irish Red from Coor's Brewing, which is actually a red lager and not an ale at all), a double red ale, an Imperial red ale, and the Belgian-style Flanders oud bruin or oud real ale. This last red style is interesting in that it is a departure from the more standard ale styles and, as a Belgian, brings many of the fruit-forward, sour characteristics of those beers but with a malt-centered approach more typical of a standard red ale.

When considering the different styles of beers favored by nano and craft brewers, Belgian-style ales and sour beers are particularly interesting, as neither really existed in any quantity in this country until the second wave of US craft brewers took hold in the early 2000s. Why? Because they're difficult to make and they bring some, let's just say, challenging flavors to the table that some might consider acquired tastes. It isn't that Americans haven't until recently been ready for the Belgians, but you probably aren't going to down a few Lambics while watching football on Sunday afternoon.

As the brewing revolution has taken off and grown in recent years, the issue for new entrants has became not how to make better beer than their rivals (that dragon had been slayed by the early microbrewers, who created more flavorful options than what was then available from the large macrobrewers) but rather how to be more unique and different than your craft competitors. The obvious first step that many took was to focus their businesses on brewing specific, hard-to-find beer styles that the other guys weren't offering.

Enter the Belgians.

Belgium and the surrounding region in Western Europe is one of the world's brewing hotbeds, home to the Trappist order of monks and the social trends that brought us Abbey-brewed beer and a number of very distinct beer styles dating back to the Middle Ages. In fact, brewing in what is now the country of Belgium can be traced back to the 1100s when, under the auspices of the Catholic Church, local monks began brewing sweet, low-alcohol beers as a substitute for drinking water in those less-than-hygienic times. These beers eventually evolved into an income source for the monasteries, as specific styles and flavors found their way into popular consumption at the time.

Today, Belgian beers for export break down into two primary categories: Trappist or Abbey beers and sours.

Trappist beers are certified as such by the International Trappist Association and must be brewed by monks within the walls of a Trappist monastery, with the proceeds going to support various social projects, to qualify for the designation. As of 2015, only ten facilities in the world qualified for this certification. Like French-made sparkling wines classified as "Champagne," based on the fact that they were produced in the Champagne region using traditional methods, Trappist beer today is a "controlled term of origin," indicating not the style of beer but rather where the beer comes from and how it's made, particularly the age-old, top-fermented brewing techniques of the Trappist monks.

Writes the International Trappist Association of its members: "The monks and nuns live according to the rule of Saint Benedict, putting the motto *'Ora et labora'* (prayer and work) into practice by producing various products which provide for their own living expenses and which also enable them to help others in need." In addition to beers, the Trappist monasteries also produce a range of "Authentic Trappist" products, including breads, cheeses, honey, liquors and wines, cosmetics, soaps, candles, supplies for religious services, and more.

As explained by the Trappist brewer Chimay, in addition to being brewed at a Trappist monastery by Trappist monks, the International Trappist Association grants the "Authentic Trappist Product" designation as a way to guarantee product origin and bases its decisions on three well-established criteria:

- "They are manufactured on-site or in close proximity to the monastery.
- The monastic community is engaged in management and all aspects of the means necessary for their operation. This must clearly reflect both the unquestionably subordinate relationship with the beneficiary monastery and the relationship with the culture of the enterprise itself in the plan of monastic life.
- The income provides for the major portion of the necessities of the community and for social services."

The six Trappist producers in Belgium (there are also two in the Netherlands, one in Austria, and one in the United States—Spencer Trappist Ale, brewed by the monks of St. Joseph's Abbey in Spencer, Massachusetts) brew a variety of different beer styles that range from blondes, to ambers, to tripels and more, all at fairly high alcohol levels and most bottle conditioned naturally, meaning they are not force carbonated before bottling, resulting in a smoother, richer mouthfeel. The best known of these in the United States is probably Chimay, which produces about 3.2 million gallons of beer each year and sells three distinct styles—Red Label, a 7 percent ABV dark; White Label, an 8 percent ABV blonde ale; and Blue Label, a 9 percent ABV dark ale—all of which are brewed at the Notre-Dame de Scourmont Abbey in the Belgian province of Hainaut. All three are sold worldwide and are generally easy to find.

Rochefort Abbey is another well-known Trappist brewery, where a handful of monks have been making beer since the sixteenth century, using water drawn from a well on-site to brew their beer. Today they sell three varieties, all darks, ranging in alcohol content from 7.5 percent to 11.3 percent. Rochefort 8, the 9.2 percent variety, is the monastery's regular production beer and is available worldwide, while Rochefort 6, at 7.5 percent ABV, is brewed just once per year.

But it's the monks at the Westvleteren Trappist brewery in Vleteren, Belgium, who have been producing beer on the grounds of the Trappist Abbey of Saint Sixtus since 1838, who have been getting most of the attention these days after their Westvleteren 12 (XII) showed up on RateBeer.com as the best beer in the world as rated by the site's users. A 10.2 percent ABV Belgian quadrupel, Westvleteren 12 (XII) is a dark brown, creamy ale heavy with raisin and prune flavors. It isn't easy to get, either. The beer is only available for purchase at the Abbey itself, and customers have to reserve their purchases in advance via the brewery's "beer phone." They don't get much choice, either, and are sold, by the case only, whatever the monks have available on the day of their visit, whether it's the 12 or not (the Westvleteren monks also brew a 5.8 percent blonde ale and an 8 percent traditional ale called Westvleteren 8).

You might think that being named "best in the world" would be great for the abbey and that the increased sales would help further support the organization's various social causes; however, the five monks who work in the brewery, according to RateBeer.com executive director, Joe Tucker, don't see it that way and were not amused by the onslaught of attention the publicity brought to their once-quiet, sedate abbey.

"One day, twenty people were there drinking the beer," Tucker told *Business Insider* in 2014 about his conversation with the monks. "The next, there's a huge line of cars waiting to buy it."

Abbey beers, on the other hand, are not required to conform to the same production standards and certifications as the Trappists. This opens up the category to monastic-style beers from a wide range of producers, including non-Trappist monks and commercial brewers. These beers are generally similar in style and preparation to their Trappist cousins—top-fermented and bottle conditioned, often dark and malty with visible yeast and high residual sugars. They also share the Trappists' usage of Belgian yeasts, in particular the *Brettanomyces* strains that produce the unique sour and banana flavors that typify Belgian beers. We'll further explore the role that these yeast strains play in terms of flavor in a later chapter.

And then we have the sours. By definition, a "sour" beer is one that is made with wild yeasts and bacteria, which introduce a range of tart and fruity flavors to a beer. Some sours accomplish this via a technique known as open fermentation, which involves leaving the wort out in the open, uncovered, throughout the fermentation process to allow whatever is floating around in the brewhouse air into the beer to give it that "wild" taste. More traditional producers don't even need to go this far, simply counting on the yeast and bacteria lurking in their aging barrels to do the work of making a beer sour. Without going into too much detail, the flavor of sour beers comes from bacteria like *Lactobacillus*, which introduces a tangy yogurt taste; *Acetobacter*, which adds a vinegar-like sourness; and the non-spore forming wild yeast strain of *Brettanomyces*, which brings funky, earthy aromas to the mix. *Brettanomyces*, or "Brett" as it is often called, is often found on the skin of fruits in the wild, and it's suspected that this is how it ended up in brewing in the first place, when brewers tried adding fruit flavors to their beers.

All the above flavors are generally considered "off" flavors in most beer styles, and wild yeasts are a full-on contaminant in most brewhouses that brewers actively work to keep out of their worts. Not so with Belgian Lambics, however, or their double-fermented cousins, the Gueuze, which blend old and young Lambics together and then bottle them for a second fermentation. Saisons and farmhouse styles also rely on wild yeasts and their associated flavors, as do those beers classified as oud bruin (literally "Old Brown" in Flemish, in reference to the fact that these Flanders brown ales age for up to a year in oak barrels) and Flanders red ale.

Either way, sour brewing can be a very unpredictable process—you never know exactly what you're going to get when working with wild yeast—and as a result, many beers of this type are blended to achieve roughly consistent results. It takes a long time, though, much longer than many other beer styles, for sours to reach maturity. So, for brewers, these beers can present a number of storage and production challenges.

These styles are, to put it mildly, different, and generally fall into the Love It or Hate It categories for many beer drinkers.

Still, they are here to stay in this country. US craft brewers have led a revival in Belgian-style ales and sour beers in recent years in their search for new and unique flavors. Not only are there now Belgian-focused brewers in cities and towns across the country, but it's also nearly impossible to go into any nanobrewery or craft brewing operation without finding at least one saison, farmhouse ale, or other Belgian-inspired beer on the menu. They're challenging to make, and they're expensive in terms of ingredients, but they're in high demand among many customers. For many brewers, this is enough of an excuse to give the style a try.

"Any brewer will tell you that these brews separate the men from the boys, the grain from the chaff, and the artists from the business-minded," wrote David Flaherty, now the marketing director for Washington State Wine and a certified cicerone, of these challenging beers on the food and beverage blog

SeriousEats.com in 2014. "While most ales take two to three weeks to produce, sours can take up to two to three years and because space in a brewery is prime real estate, having this stuff just sitting around, totally unsure if it's ever going to amount to anything delicious is a gamble. And much like in the movie *Outbreak*, if these wild bugs get loose in your brewery and spread over your equipment, you're in for one hell of a crime scene cleanup . . . and Morgan Freeman ain't gonna save you. Wineries and breweries go to great lengths to keep Brett and Lacto far away, so just bringing them into your operation is a huge risk. But, the glory is legendary. Breweries that can successfully conquer this category sit at the top, revered by all who attempted and failed, or who didn't have the *chutzpah* to step onto the field."

And the exploration of style and flavor among these brewers does not end with beers. Ginger ales, barleywines, hard ciders, and more are all fair game for craft and nanobrewers, provided they still process more or less like beer (thereby using the same equipment) and can be made commercially viable.

"Myself and my business partner, we're currently working on Denver's first sake brewery," graphic designer Marc Hughes tells me as we sit at the bar at the Denver Bicycle Café, a beer-centric bar and bike shop east of downtown. "We're working through a bunch of the legal stuff right now to get it so we can start selling it, but we have all that stuff moving forward and have been in production now for a few months."

I met Hughes through the incubator program at Grandma's House, where Hughes and his partners had been working to perfect their recipes on Fuerst's system in late 2014. Sake, best known as a near-ubiquitous Japanese beverage enjoyed both hot and cold, goes through a very beer-like lagering process, using rice as the base "malt" instead of barley or cereal grains. Like beer, the process involves pulling the natural starches from a wort-like mixture and then allowing yeast to convert those sugars into alcohol. Unlike beer, however, the rice base used in sake brewing releases its sugars directly during the boil stage (rather than going from a multistep process from starch to sugar to alcohol), allowing sakes to be made with as much as 20 percent ABV, though it is commonly diluted down to 15 to 17 percent for sale. It's a slow, cold fermentation process that takes about two-and-a-half months from start to finish (compare that to just a few weeks for many beers), with about six weeks of actual fermenting and the rest of the time being used to age the sake. Unlike beer, sake comes out of the fermentation stage with what many people consider a "green flavor," due to excess acidity. Aging it for a few weeks helps to mellow out that flavor.

When I met Hughes, only a handful of domestic sake producers operated in the United States, including Moto-I in Minneapolis, Minnesota; Ben's American Sake Brewery in Asheville, North Carolina; and Texas Sake, in Austin, Texas. Portland's SakeOne is the largest domestic sake producer by volume, having gotten its start in 1992 as a sake importer. Compare that to more than 1,700 at the time in Japan, exporting more than 3.7 million gallons in 2012, according to Japan's Ministry of Agriculture, Forestry, and Fisheries. Sure, the sake in the market in the United States was (and largely still is) miniscule when compared to Japan, where the average adult downs just over two gallons of the drink every year. But for many sake producers in this country, all they see is a huge opportunity for growth, both among Japanese expats in the United States as well as American drinkers who have yet to discover sake.

Best of all, competition in the niche is nowhere near what craft and nanobrewers are now experiencing.

"I wouldn't want to be opening a brewery now," Jonathan Robinson, the owner and brewer of Ben's American Sake told NPR in 2013. "Everyone is making beer now, and here a lot of people have been brewing for twenty years. But with sake, we're breaking new ground."

Hughes, who had pieced together his own sake education in the early days by scouring the Internet for basic recipes and sourcing ingredients through enthusiast groups, agrees.

"We're kind of starting off at the same position as a lot of the beer companies did about ten years ago," he says. "For us, the whole process involves breaking down all of these little components of flavor and figuring out how they all work; why this one is good and why that one is not good."

He's doing that by developing a number of different sakes based around the American palate. While most of the Japanese sakes we order at restaurants and have access to in this country fit the tastes of Japanese customers, generally offering sweet and dry varieties, no one has yet found a sake style that really appeals to American tastes the way beer and wine do. So, as opposed to the more traditional styles, Hughes and his partners have been trying to take some of the more obscure Japanese styles—like black rice sake and red rice sake—in the hopes that these more interesting sakes will be a better fit for the American palate. They are also trying some oak-aged sakes that tend to be a little more whiskey-esque without the burn of a strong, distilled liquor.

"So we're trying to make it, for lack of a better term, more of a PBR sort of thing," Hughes says about his efforts at an "everyday American" sake. "So it's what American taste buds know, more than say the fruitier or floral stuff of traditional Japanese sakes."

Part of the goal, he explains, is to take sake out of the Japanese restaurant setting that most people are familiar with and introduce it as something that can be enjoyed with a wide range of foods and in a wide range of settings. It's something that others in the food-and-beverage industry have been working on for years—introducing sake pairings for grilled meat plates and noodle dishes, rather than just focusing on it as something that's enjoyed with sushi and that's it. One of the red sakes that Hughes's team makes, for instance, uses a sweet mead yeast instead of the standard red rice yeast, which gives it a more acidic, almost cider-like flavor that's more savory than traditional sakes. That allows it to pair well with heavier flavors like red meat dishes or spiced meats.

"We're trying to break away from the idea that this has to be served with sushi, so we're pairing it with hamburgers and other typically American style foods. Some of the flavor profiles work for that."

And, like a beer brewer, he eventually hopes to have sake styles to fit a wide range of flavor needs.

"It's like switching from like a pilsner or a light lager when you're having burgers to something that's more like a stout or an amber or has a complementary flavor profile for other foods," he says. "It will be an education process but we're getting there."

CHAPTER 6

PROCESS

"You're all wanking sissies if you even think about using a grain mill, teeth, or ball-peen hammer. A real brewer uses 17 vestal virgins stomping on the grain in a large wooden vat. And yeast is for losers. True brewers just dip one end of their dog into the wort to get things going."

—Drew Avis, founder, StrangeBrew brewing software

Roughly translated, the term *de steeg* means "the alley" in Dutch, and that's exactly where you'll find De Steeg Brewing: facing onto an alley on Denver's far north side.

Outside, nothing much indicates that the place itself is a brewery—just some glass doors and a nondescript black-and-white sign give away what the low-slung, gray cinderblock structure does not. At first glance, it looks more like a garage than anything else, and not a very nice one at that.

It's located in the midst of a rapidly gentrifying neighborhood, though, so what was once a quiet stretch of auto shops and Mexican restaurants is fast being taken over by craft beer bars, boutiques, and high-end dining options. Directly across from De Steeg (where there were once, as in just a few years ago, a line of 1930s-era brick bungalows), are now half a dozen, brand-new two-story modern duplexes, looming over the alley with their wood and metal facades. Garage doors open to reveal various shades of Mercedes, BMW, and Audi SUVs.

The taproom itself does have an address—4342 Tennyson Street—that corresponds with the street behind the facility, which makes finding the place the first time something of an adventure and, laughs owner Craig Rothgery, helps keep foot traffic to a minimum. You come to De Steeg because you've heard about it, you know it is here, and you want to see what all of the fuss is about.

But, like many off-the-beaten-path food and drink providers, once you make it to the taproom, the effort pays off. Founded by Rothgery as a one-man operation in 2013, De Steeg is a 1.25-barrel nanobrewery (yes, one-and-a-quarter-barrel) specializing in Belgian-inspired beer styles, all crammed into a thirty-three-person space that's finished in dark woods and fabrics, with a long oak bar and a scattering of high-top tables. And, given the small system he's working on, Rothgery likes to brew a lot of small batches and experiment with his recipes, rather than dial in the same thing time after time. For instance, he had brewed his hundredth different recipe by the time I met with him, just about two years after opening his doors.

"I do love Belgian beers, but it's not what I focus on," Rothgeny told the *Denver Post*'s beer blog, *First Drafts*, ahead of his 2013 opening. "I think it's pretty obvious I don't have a focus."

One thing many of the recipes at De Steeg do have in common, though, is high alcohol content and strong flavors.

"I have a tendency to err toward the higher alcohol stuff—8 percent and above," Rothgeny admitted to the newspaper. "I just like bolder, bigger beers. I don't think I make hop bombs. I like to do balanced beers."

For example, although the tap list at De Steeg changes from day to day, he does have some favorites that rotate in more often than not.*

On a recent visit, Rothgery's three-person staff was pouring eight different beers, including a 9.0 percent ABV French saison that's described as "slightly sweet," a 10 percent ABV Belgian Special Dark, and an 8 percent ABV Oak Aged Belgian Red that Rothgery described as a "crisp red with a light sour note." His "house ale"—named Het Huis, which is Dutch for "the house"—is a slightly malty and sweet Belgian-inspired ale (and generally the only selection that Rothgery keeps on tap at all times, and even that clocks in at nearly 9 percent ABV, as does the Gewurztraminer Ale, a tart beer/wine hybrid). Even De Steeg's lighter selections—including a Belgian Wit, Summer Rye Ale, and Ginger-infused Ale—bring some pretty heavy-hitting flavors to the table. These are not beers for wallflowers.

---

* If you like something on the menu, it's best to get a growler of it to go right away because you never know when it's going to run out. His 1.25-barrel system can only produce enough beer for about two-and-a-half full-sized kegs at a time.

Rothgery himself got into the brewing business after a career as a mechanical engineer, working on food systems for both Nestlé (where he helped design the machines used to make Hot Pockets) and Gallo Wines. An active homebrewer for years, he says his engineering background has given him a unique view on the systems and processes that go into brewing beer and have helped him create his DIY brewery in ways that many other brewers may not be able.

"I'm always shocked that people who are not engineers get into [brewing] because there's so much with this that's engineering related, like process engineering," Rothgery told me as we sat at De Steeg's dark pine bar, looking back into the small brewhouse. "I designed process skids for Gallo Wineries and stuff like that, so I'm very familiar with the process of brewing. And I did build all this stuff from scratch in my garage; I essentially welded it all up."

Honestly, he says, as a customer, he can tell now when he goes into a brewery—nano or not—that's been set up by an engineer versus one where the brewer doesn't have that background. On the one hand, you can look around a well-done brewhouse and see exactly how everything works and where everything is going—a very flow-centric design is clear and thought-out. On the other hand, sometimes you look at someone else's brewery and have to ask yourself, "What were they thinking?"

"They essentially just crammed equipment into a space with no rhyme or reason," he says. "So it's very obvious when you see someone who knows the manufacturing world and sets up their brewery that way."

Given his own background, it should come as no surprise that Rothgery set up his brewhouse with this type of process flow in mind. As of early 2015, he was working on what he considered to be the smallest system in Denver, and in one of the smallest commercial brewing spaces, but everything was organized in such a way that it didn't feel as small as it really was. He had opened on what looked, at first glance, to be a plastic-bottle system (the bottles were used for fermentation) before eventually upgrading to a stainless steel system, also of his own design.

"I had eight fermenters before and it was really nice having the eight," he says. "It gave me a lot of time since fermenter space was not my bottleneck.

Actually kicking kegs was my bottleneck, which was a really nice problem to have. I'm trying to see if I can make do with four right now. It's tight. We're moving beer sometimes a little bit faster than I would like. So, you know, it's not a bad thing, just not ideal."

Still, Rothgery says he does not feel too held back by his small system. Rather, he sees brewing on a larger system as more time consuming since, at that scale, your transfer times between each of the steps—pumping wort between vessels and waiting as everything heats up—are longer. He's better able to dial in his process to minimize the overall time frame of his brews. When I visited De Steeg, he and his staff were only brewing about once a week, on Tuesdays, and were able to do double-batches on that schedule, enough to serve their taproom needs for the week. Expanding into outside distribution, however, likely would have called for more production.

The fact is, he says, the actual process time for brewing a batch of beer is roughly the same no matter what size the brewery is. You're still mashing for an hour, you're still boiling for an hour, you're still adding hops on a set schedule, so those times are pretty consistent no matter what scale the brewer is working at. It's just a matter of how much time it takes to move the liquids around and how much time it takes to heat everything up; those are the kinds of bottlenecks that large brewing operations have to deal with. Brewing on an underpowered system in terms of heat output, he says, can be a huge drag on time.

And that's where engineering often enters into the process.

"Yeah, a lot of places will put some good environmental practices in place, like the water they use to cool the beer they'll put back into their hot water for their mash for the next day. That saves a lot of energy."

At De Steeg, he's not able to do that because of space limitations, so he literally has to pour hot water down the drain, losing a lot of the energy (in the form of electrical heat generation) that he spends money to create. On a small scale like a nanobrewery, that may not be such a big deal, but as commercial operations grow, it becomes more and more important and is the type of inefficiency that brewery designers look to eliminate as they optimize their systems. So, by the time he's done transferring his mash, his wort is almost to a boil—it only takes a couple minutes, which might be better even than the times I get on my stovetop at home—and that helps condense his overall brew times. But every brew system is different. In some places, the boil might be ready to rock in just a few minutes, whereas others have an undersized boiler and don't have the steam pressure they need, so the process just takes them a little bit longer.

"Brewing isn't difficult, the actual act of brewing," Rothgery says. "It's very assembly worker–esque. You go into Great Divide or any of those places and the brewers are following their worksheet, adding ingredients at specific times, hitting temperatures and hitting buttons. There's not a whole lot of art to it. That's why everyone has started talking about the true craft breweries where it's much more manual and it's more dynamic. That's why I only have two regulars [on tap]. I really don't want to make the same beer over and over. It just gets really boring."

As discussed previously, the brewing process has changed very little over the centuries. The basic ingredients—water, grains, yeast, and hops—remain the same. And the steps involved—mashing the grains into wort, boiling the mix, adding some flavoring agents, pitching the yeast, and fermenting it all together—are just as they always have been. Even the packaging and sale of commercial beer has been consistent for a long time: the last true "innovation" in beer packaging was the evolution of the aluminum can in the 1960s. (In fact, Colorado-based Coors Brewing was the first to introduce the all-aluminum, seamless, two-piece beverage container, according to the Aluminum Association, rolling out the first cans in 1959 and paying a return fee of one cent for each can that was returned to the brewery for reuse. Royal Crown Cola brought canning to the soft drink market in 1964.)

What that means is that, even as the landscape of brewing has grown and changed throughout the years, with changing styles coming into vogue and new techniques being used, the basic hardware of the business has remained fairly consistent. Today, most everything in a modern brewery is made of stainless steel that, in addition to being strong enough to stand up to the demands of commercial manufacturing, is also nonreactive and therefore easy to sterilize and keep clean. Plastic, also nonreactive, piping is used to transport liquids between each of the steps in the process, while an array of digital sensors and controllers not only can monitor the recipe as it takes shape but, at some larger breweries, even manage the brewing process automatically—turning valves on and off, activating heating elements, adding hops, and more—taking the human brewer out of the equation almost entirely. (That is not the case at the nano and small-scale neighborhood operations profiled in this book, for the record, where the hands-on, manual craft of brewing is part of the business plan and a large part what sets them apart.) Finally, chemical cleaners and power scrubbers ensure that all the equipment used in modern brewing is properly cleaned between batches, all but eliminating the threat of a contamination issue ruining a batch of beer.

Clearly, today's brewers enjoy some technological advantages over their forefathers, in terms of both hardware and system designs. Like everything else in modern life, technology has transformed the brewing industry. It's just that, in this case, many of the advances happened well before the modern information age got started.

For instance, prior to the last couple of centuries, brewers struggled to produce consistent, quality beers given all the variables they were forced to address during the brewing process—from unstable heating sources, to questionable ingredients, to unreliable sterilization methods. The introduction of James Watt's steam-driven engine in 1775 helped address some of the variables by enabling brewers to, for the first time, install automated features like stirring mechanisms and boil timers in their facilities. This not only ensured better, more consistent mixing during the boil process, but it also allowed brewers to eventually scale up their production levels, as they were no longer limited by pure human effort to power their breweries.

The next step in the development of brewing technology came in 1871, when Carl von Linde introduced refrigeration to the world, allowing brewers to dial in exactly the temperature they needed to optimize the performance of their recipes and ensuring the availability of low-term storage for the final product. Prior to this, beer was primarily brewed in the winter because heat-sensitive yeast made it very difficult to achieve desirable results in the warmer months. Brewers simply made enough each winter to get through the summer, storing it in underground cellars to keep cool, before repeating the process when temperatures fell again the next fall. Obviously, this limitation was not ideal for commercial production. But large-scale refrigeration changed all that, making it possible to brew beer year-round and better control the temperature during the process.

Perhaps most importantly, however, was French microbiologist Louis Pasteur's identification in 1857 of yeast as the driving force in alcohol creation. This fully (and finally) unlocked the secrets of the fermentation process, not only bringing true understanding to the long-mysterious process, but also giving brewers access to new tools to manipulate and perfect the art of fermentation in their own beers. Through Pasteur's research, we learned that yeast cells—which had first been identified in beer by Dutch scientist Anton Van Leeuwenhoek in 1680, using a primitive microscope—are living microorganisms in their own right and that, by acting on other cells, they are able to produce chemical changes that include the creation of alcohol, souring in milk, lift in bread as it is baked, and others. Pasteur published these findings in his 1877 "Studies on Fermentation" but was never able to isolate the specific yeast enzyme that causes fermentation. That would have to wait until 1897, when Eduard Buechner, a German chemist, found that by grinding up yeast particles in a sort of juice, he was able to ferment liquids just as with live yeast cells. His findings, which won him the 1907 Nobel Prize in Chemistry, eventually allowed brewers to isolate specific yeast cultures based on their fermentation characteristics, creating the landscape of established brewing yeasts that we know today.

(Pasteur, for his part, was not a one-and-done scientist. Among his other discoveries, Pasteur is also credited with groundbreaking work in vaccination, germ theory, and pasteurization, the process of food preservation named after him.)

In terms of hardware, the widespread adoption of corrosion-resistant stainless steel in the early twentieth century changed food and beverage production forever, enabling all sorts of manufacturers—brewers included—to produce more consistent, higher-quality products at scale and not be held back by the cleaning and sanitation limitations of fragile copper, iron, and other vessels. Stainless steel is made, to put it simply, with a high percentage (10 percent or more) of chromium mixed with low-carbon, making it unique in its ability to both resist stains and corrosion as well as effectively heal itself due to the chromium content in the metal. Exposure to oxygen activates a reaction in the chromium oxide on the surface of the metal, repairing minor nicks and scrapes as well as chemical damage to the surface itself. With more than sixty different grades currently on the market with different corrosion-resistance properties based on the other elements used in the blend, modern stainless steel is a good looking, corrosion-resistant metal widely used in manufacturing due to its ease in cleaning and sterilizing. It also offers a surprisingly high strength-to-weight ratio, meaning that less of it is needed when compared to equipment made from lower-quality metals.

For brewers, especially small brewers where the brewhouse is often on-site at the taproom, there is another advantage here: good looks. Shiny, gleaming stainless steel brew tanks look nice behind the bar and lend the operation a look of quality, of space-age class. Sure, traditional copper kettles might look sharp (though even the copper vessels used at larger, touring breweries are often just there for looks, and the tanks themselves are most often copper-coated stainless steel for the performance reasons noted previously), but they are hard to maintain and finicky to work with. Stainless is just the better option.

So what does all this cost? A lot. Certainly, costs vary widely between equipment providers and breweries, but as a general rule, professional-grade commercial systems at the three-barrel level start around $10,000 and go up quickly from there. And that's for a fairly basic, two-vessel, gas-fired system with no extra control or automation add-ons: just a hot liquor tank, brew kettle, and wort chiller with all the necessary burners, gauges, clamps, valves, and hoses to set it up and start brewing.

Beyond that, though, the sky is almost literally the limit. For example, Brew Stuff is a custom fabricator of brewhouse equipment specializing in the home-brew and small craft brewing markets. Its complete systems, which range in size from one-barrel all the way up to ten barrels as predesigned systems, cost between roughly $4,000 and $67,000 based solely on the size of the system and the equipment needed for each. The company's gas-fired ten-barrel system, for example, is a two-vessel, dome-topped stainless steel setup with a built-in firebox for even heating throughout the tanks and upgrade options, including a larger wort chiller and an automated temperature control system at about $1,500 each. Its top-of-the-line system includes all-electric controls and a steam-heated brewing system.

What does the typical nanobrewer really need in terms of brewhouse equipment? As with everything, it depends on the size of the operation they want to build. At its highest level, a typical commercial brewery needs a few standard things in its facility to successfully brew beer:

Storage: Brewing at the commercial level calls for large amounts of base malt, dried hops, and other ingredients, all of which needs to be stored somewhere until it is time to brew. On the flip side, finished beer needs to be stored both as it goes through the fermentation process (in fermentation tanks) or in barrels if long-term aging is desired.

Water: Although it doesn't need to be stored on-site, access to a high-volume water source is critical to the success of any brewery, no matter how small. A hot liquor tank is where the brewer heats up their sparge water during the mash process, so there needs to either be space for that vessel or access to on-demand hot water from another source, such as a tankless water heater, on-site.

Brewing vessels: This is where it all happens. Typically, most nanobrewers work on two-vessel systems, but three-vessel setups are not uncommon and

allow for better isolation of steps in the process. And, as discussed previously, capacity varies from brewhouse to brewhouse, but technically most nanos are built around three-barrel or smaller systems.

Process controls: At the commercial level, there is far more to the brewing process than just making wort and filling kegs. Liquids need to be heated, cooled, measured, and moved from tank to tank. Electrical control systems are now available to handle many of these chores.

Sizing up over time is possible, but many of the brewers and suppliers I spoke with don't recommend it, primarily because it isn't as easy as just buying a larger mash tun and calling it a day. So many parts of the brewing process are interconnected that increasing the size of one piece effectively requires large pieces throughout. It can't be done one at a time. Granted, this isn't universally true. There are several steps in the process, fermentation tanks are one example, where equipment can be scaled up or down based on volume needs (whether or not the brewer plans to bottle, for instance, or distribute kegs of their beer to local restaurants and bars) or available floor space. But most of the decisions on system size come down to simple dollars and cents. How much capital is available for the brewhouse, and how much can they afford to spend before opening their doors? For nanobrewers, this hurdle often isn't as steep as it seems—after all, part of the point of running a nano operation is the small size that keeps costs down—but there are still some significant costs involved.

For instance, Las Vegas Stainless & Copper Works advertises a two-vessel, three-barrel, self-contained nano brewhouse for $14,000 that, they say, offers startup brewers a turnkey system that's effectively ready to brew on delivery. Built out and installed, the brewer is likely looking at about a $20,000 investment. The company, which designs and manufactures everything it sells in-house, offers systems ranging in size from half-barrel up to forty-barrel, depending on the needs of its brewery clients, and can build systems based on either individual vessels or "plug and brew" systems based around skidded hardware that can be swapped out or added to an existing brewhouse as needed.

"A lot of the nano guys are coming from a homebrewing background and, you know, they're pretty strapped for cash," explains Shane Surber, the owner of Las Vegas Stainless & Copper Works. "So it's the single-wall, kettle style, professional system that most of them want right now. And then I get a few guys who want that real professional-grade brewpub setup. They have the capital to really put together a solid cash based setup."

His basic three-barrel system, for example, is a gas-heated unit aimed at nanobrewers that includes a mash/lauter tun, boil kettle/whirlpool, burner control system, a magnetic drive beer pump, wort chiller, and all the cabling, sensors, valves, fittings, and tubing needed to get everything up and running. It is essentially a homebrew setup that's stepped up with professional quality components, including single-wall kettles, centrifugal pumps, plate-frame heat exchangers, and all stainless steel construction.

The price difference between that type of brewhouse system and a more professional brewpub setup, he says, starts at about $15,000, with the higher end options going for around $40,000 and the more basic versions falling in the mid-$20s range, depending on the options chosen.

From there, brewers can choose their individual components if they want to—a separate mash tun and whirlpool, for example, rather than using the same vessel for both stages—or more automation, depending on the size of their operation and how much beer they need to make. There's a limit to how much "upscaling" is possible, however. It's possible to improve production by incorporating a separate whirlpool, for example, or adding another oil kettle to the standard two-vessel brewhouse that he sells. But the fact is that a three-barrel system is a three-barrel system, regardless of the price or sophistication level of the hardware. There's really no getting around that limitation. ("It's the same for the fifteen," Surber laughs, "A fifteen is a fifteen, you can't make it into a thirty.")

The most efficient brewhouse in terms of total volume at this level would be a four-vessel setup that has a separate mash tun, a separate lauder tun, a separate oil kettle, and a separate whirlpool, but that is often beyond the means of most startup operators, both in terms of startup capital and brewhouse space. The truth is, a brewer can start out with a two-vessel system that

combines some of these functions and step up some of the individual pieces as their budget allows. Granted, this really only improves production and process flow, it doesn't add output capacity, but such upgrades can make the brewer's life—which at the small scale of nanobrewers often includes brewing multiple batches back to back to keep up with demand—a little bit easier. Stepping up to a larger system in terms of capacity involves, not surprisingly, investing in a larger system.

"There's definitely a lot of interest in the nanos right now," Surber says. "There are probably a hundred quotations for these small systems that I've sent out. It just takes time, you know, between all the licensing and the trademarks and all the things that you have to do to get a brewery up and running. It's a lot of work, but the nano market is going to be very, very big. As far as the brewing goes, I think it will go back to what it was before Prohibition where it was really a small local thing, and you'll see a lot of small, local businesses doing it. I think that's where it's going to go."

Tim Moore, the owner of Colorado Brewing Systems, a nano-focused brewhouse fabricator in Fort Collins, knows this all too well. In addition to his equipment business, he's the founder and owner of Freedom's Edge Brewing Company in Cheyenne, Wyoming, about an hour north of Fort Collins, just over the state line. Even located that close to one of the hottest small cities in craft beer, however, Wyoming is still something of an undiscovered country for brewers, and Moore knew that going in (in fact, when he opened his doors, there was only one other operating brewpub in the city). Since opening in 2012, he has moved the operation from the historic Tivoli Building in downtown Cheyenne, a holdover from the area's days as a frontier stopover, to a larger production facility on the north side of town, an indication of how much pent-up demand there was (and still is) for craft beer in the Cowboy State.

He knows how tough it can be for brewers at this level, too. After opening a second location of Freedom's Edge in Fort Collins, he was forced to shutter it after less than a year. Turned out, the three-barrel system he installed was only capable of providing enough beer for the taproom itself and was limiting the business's growth potential. "After going for a while [in Fort Collins], we realized we needed to start distribution, and we can't do it in this space," Shane O'Keefe, Moore's son-in-law who comanages the brewery operations, told the *Coloradoan* newspaper at the time. "There's plenty of room in [the Cheyenne brewery], so we can start distributing there and then look into Colorado."

But Moore is still a nanobrewer at heart, working on a three-barrel system he designed and built himself. In fact, the experience of sourcing the brewhouse equipment for Freedom's Edge, especially the costs involved, are what got him into the equipment side of the business in the first place.

"We did everything ourselves," he says, "but we kind of were pushed into that situation because some of the solutions out there were so far out of what our price range was for starting a brewery based on a three-barrel system. And when you start looking at all the little pieces that need to come together, they add up pretty quickly."

It made sense for him personally, too, given that his professional background was in manufacturing and heavy industry. In addition to his work as an active homebrewer for the better part of two decades, prior to moving to Colorado, Moore owned an electronic security business in Indiana that manufactured control components for residential and commercial systems. Before that, he was a stainless steel welder.

"So all of the pieces sort of fell into place," he laughs, "and everything I needed to do this business it turned out I have the experience for."

These days, in addition to the brewery, he fabricates systems for small startup brewers and what he calls the "advanced homebrew market," those folks who have been brewing on their own for a while and want to explore the possibility of doing something at a commercial level. They may not be ready to make the jump just yet but want some higher-quality equipment to maybe get them there and eventually serve as a pilot system or small component of a full-sized, commercial brewhouse. The line, as he sees it, is homebrewers at the twenty- to forty-gallon level—most starter homebrew systems are five gallons, so these are high-level private brewers—that's when people start looking for the upgrade options that he offers, which include stainless steel components and higher-end fittings.

"One of the big areas where we've been successful is our turnkey half-barrel and one-barrel systems," Moore says. "And there you're looking somewhere between $2,700 to $5,700 to at least get to that stage. And then it takes a pretty big bump when you're going to a three-barrel, because we do a lot of the electrical controllers and other options that are really starting to become popular on the nano-sized systems. There you're looking at $4,000 to $5,000 just for the controls, and that's even before you add the tanks or anything else."

Those electrical systems, although they can be pricey, are becoming popular among small brewers, too, he says, in part because they eliminate the hassle of working with gas, so the brewer doesn't have to worry about venting or some of the installation costs associated with all of that. Other upgrades that Moore sees a lot are automation system add-ons and commercial grade tankless water heaters to eliminate the need for a hot liquor tank. Those run about $1,200 each plus installation, and most brewers need to run two or more in parallel to get the flow rate they need for production, but the savings of not having an extra tank and one less control stage generally work out as a cost savings overall. It also adds an extra layer of speed and efficiency to the brewing operation, not to mention saving space in the brewhouse.

Even software is making inroads in the brewing industry, with a range of brewhouse management programs currently on the market and more appearing seemingly every day. One such option, installed in some 160 breweries as of 2015, is called OrchestratedBeer and it is positioned as a brewery management solution that brings together everything an owner needs to track and optimize their business in one place, including everything from accounting, to inventory management, to production, to purchasing, sales, quality control, and more. It is available as a cloud-based service for a monthly subscription fee or as a stand-alone software product for enterprise users (i.e., larger breweries). And that's just one example. Similar setups are available from VicinityBrew, BeerRun, Ekos Brewmaster, BrewMan, and SWK's BrewX, all of which take a top-down look at the business overall, much as inventory and workflow management software programs function in other industries.

On the flip side, BrewSoft is a software product I saw in action at Fiction Brewing that focuses entirely on the brewing process itself, with no features to manage the business side of the house. It, and other programs like it, allow the brewer to monitor the steps of the process in real time, loading their recipe into the system and letting it tell them how long to boil, what specific gravity numbers to look for, when to add each round of hops, etc. Matthew Fuerst has a similar system installed at Grandma's House, allowing him to punch in a recipe on a wall-mounted template and effectively walk away, allowing the system to prepare the proper amount of water and bring it up to the needed temperature. When it's ready, he can add his malts to the mash and walk through the process with the help of this software "brewmaster" keeping him informed of the steps. And this is not just a craft beer thing—a program called Brewmaxx, for instance, provides similar services and is widely used by macrobrewers including Anheuser-Busch, Heineken, Carlsberg, Tsingtao, and more.

But for all the enthusiasm currently surrounding the nanobrewing side of the craft beer market, there are some dissenting voices, particularly when it comes to the equipment needed to set up and run a profitable brewery. It's no secret that brewing on a tiny system is a lot of work and often requires that the brewer make multiple batches of beer each week just to keep up with demand. What's less often talked about, however, are the constraints that a small system like this places on a startup business's aspirations overall.

"In 24 years in this industry, we have seen NO evidence that a start-up microbrewery (meaning primarily wholesale sales, NOT a brewpub) is a viable business at less than 10 barrel size, and more realistically 15 barrel MINIMUM size," writes Sound Brewing Systems, a seller of new and used brewery equipment in Olympia, Washington, on its website. "A micro will not become consistently profitable until it produces some thousands of barrels per year . . . 3,000 or so is a ballpark number. You can't get there with a 3 or 4 barrel system. Do the math."

Harsh words, for sure, but they raise a key concern that all potential nanobrewers must consider when planning their businesses and their equipment purchases. If, as Sound Brewing Systems asserts, a startup brewpub needs to sell at least five hundred barrels of beer in-house to be self-sustaining in terms

of revenue, if not outright successful as a business, and that a seven-barrel system, at minimum, is needed to make this happen without tying the brewer to their system 24/7, is it even worth trying to make a go of it on a three-barrel? Are nanobrewers setting themselves up to fail? Further, given the cost of production on these small systems, the supplier says that many brewers would be further ahead to simply buy wholesale kegged beer from a craft beer distributor rather than try and make it themselves at the nano level and would likely end up making around the same profit if they did.

"A 3 or 4 barrel microbrewery (wholesale production) is doomed to either fail, or enslave its operator with interminable hours and little compensation until he can upgrade his equipment to a large enough system to become profitable on," the company writes. "In many instances the venture self destructs and visits financial ruin upon the owner."

Why do nanobreweries even exist, then? One consideration that Sound Brewing Systems, and others who share its worldview, do not take into account when calculating the cost of production on small systems? Labor. True, paying a brewery staff to brew beer on a nano system may well be cost prohibitive for a startup, but the fact is that more nanobreweries are run by owner-operators. They are able to control their labor costs by absorbing them as the brewer and business owner themselves. For example, Ryan Kilpatrick of Fiction Brewing employs an assistant brewer but handles most of the heavy lifting associated with the process himself (on top of his "other" full-time career as an accountant). That, and the fact that his wife, Christa, also works behind the bar, further deflates their labor tab. What's more, brewers like the Kilpatricks are able to justify higher prices for their beers at the consumer level—$5 and $6 pints are not uncommon—due to the exclusivity of their product and the rates the market overall has established for small, local, craft beer. That further helps revenues by boosting the profit that a small, neighborhood brewer can make on each keg of beer it sells. Macrobrewers, and even larger craft brewers and brewpubs, don't always enjoy that same pricing advantage.

Make no mistake, though, nanobrewing is a financially risky and low-margin business. But, like every small business, there are ways for founders and brewers to make a go of it, profitably, despite the challenges and limitations of working on small systems.

And then there's Josh Van Riper's Odyssey Beerwerks in suburban Arvada, Colorado.

Built into a double-wide space in an industrial park about fifteen miles northwest of Denver, roughly half of Odyssey's space is set aside for the tap-room—complete with a hardwood bar and a few dozen tables opposite near floor-to-ceiling windows—while the rest is taken up by the brewhouse itself. And it's big, just over four thousand square feet with soaring thirty-foot ceilings; plenty of room, as Van Riper later tells me, for three to four times as many fermenters and other pieces of hardware that he already has. As it stands, Odyssey's setup includes a fifteen-barrel brewhouse, four fifteen-barrel fermenters, and two thirty-barrel fermenters, meaning it's capable of fermenting 120 barrels at any one time. He can also can his beers on-site.

Aside from all the gleaming stainless steel, however, the thing that stands out most about Odyssey's brewhouse is how organized it is. In addition to the lineup of brew kettles and fermenters, which are standard issue at every brewery, Van Riper and co-owner Chris Hill created a very "flow centric" brewing operation, with a grain storage vessel, hot and cold water lines, drainage pipes, and other process aides laid out in a very clean, logical way. Even as an outsider, it's very easy to look at the system and see how everything comes together, how it gets from point A to point B and where it all ends up. Less noticeable are the wiring and control systems, also all developed by the owners, which enable the staff to remotely manage the fermenters and other vessels throughout the brewing process.

"So we did all of the glycol ourselves in here," Van Riper tells me as we tour the brewhouse, him pointing out all the components he either designed or built himself before the brewery opened in 2013, "and pretty much everything that's back behind here, which is hot and cold water and all that."

The lines themselves run far overhead, snaking between the various pieces of brewing equipment and connecting to each of the vessels a good fifteen feet above the ground.

Van Riper, a twenty-year mechanical engineering professional with a background in systems engineering and electrical systems, also built a keg washer and modified an automated canning line to work for the brewery's packaging operation. (Odyssey was canning about forty-five cases per hour when I visited and was selling its beer across Colorado, with national expansion already in its sights.) It started out as a two-head manual system, he says, but it has evolved over time to include more automated features as he has time to work on it. "I'm working on the fill heads now, and I've got this new style fill head that I've put in there. As a matter of fact, tomorrow I'm canning and I'm going to add in a CO_2 foam injection just to see how that does with the foam on top."

He also designed a large steel grain storage bin—something he referred to as "a pretty easy project, honestly"—where the malts could wait between milling and brewing, with piping to take them to the mash tun when needed. That way, when the staff started brewing in the morning, the grains prepared the day before could easily be sent straight over to the kettle with the necessary hot water to start the mash.

"We don't have any capacity problems on the brew side," he says. "When you're brewing a 15-barrel batch, it's pretty easy to keep up. We've got 120 barrels of fermentation space right now and that's growing, but it'll be a while before we have to worry about upgrading the brewhouse, and that was the plan from the beginning."

Van Riper's old homebrewing setup, also a very DIY project with a welded steel support system for the various buckets and pipes, sits amidst all of this commercial brewing equipment, serving these days as a pilot system for the brewery.

"What's funny, if you really look at that homebrew system versus the main brew aisle that we have over there now, there's three big vessels on the one side and three little ones on the other," he says. "And you've got your mash tun, your kettle, and your hot liquor tank on both sides. So the brewing process is remarkably the same. Fermentation, these are essentially giant carboys over here, so that isn't all that different either, except that it's a lot easier to chill these to the right temperature than it is when you're doing it at home."

It is, in fact, the same system that Van Riper built for his homebrew hobby back in the early 1990s, just much, much bigger. He spent a lot of time shopping for parts this time around, he admits, choosing components that would work well together and cherry-picking everything for his brewhouse along the way. His engineering background came into play when it was time to connect the pieces and make sure it all worked as expected. This turned out to be a good way for the startup operation to save money—buying piecemeal from the suppliers who could offer the best prices on everything they needed—but it also allowed them to build the system that would best meet their needs, both at the start as well as down the road.

They went with a fifteen-barrel system from day one, he says, because they didn't want to have to go through a growth spurt three to five years in and be forced to rebuild it. True, it's a very large system for a local brewery (and, if we're using the strict definition of a nanobrewery here, it doesn't even qualify for the label) but, given the company's goals, they decided it would be a better investment to start as an undersized operation on a larger system for the first few years versus having to play catch-up as the business grew. Van Riper says Odyssey is on a steady growth plan through the first five years, and the plan includes expanding to new markets and going out of state in the near term. It is very difficult to support that kind of growth on a smaller system.

"At the size like what Craig's got [at De Steeg] it's tough to make that switch from small brewer to distributor because if you start selling a lot of product, yeah that's fine, but you're not going to get there if it's just kegs. It's really hard to sell a lot of keg products since the draft stuff is really hard to break into. It's a lot easier to sell to liquor stores right now, but I think that'll change later on."

Both experienced homebrewers and Colorado natives, Van Riper and Hill had known each other for decades before deciding to go into business together (hence the name, the creation of Odyssey Beerwerks was an odyssey in its own right). Brewing was a logical choice, though, because it leveraged everything

they already knew how to do, including Van Riper's engineering and systems background. Hill, for his part, left a twenty-year career in marketing and advertising to start Odyssey, though he admits those skills are still put to use on a daily basis at the brewery. After that kind of time in other careers, the transition to brewing entrepreneurs has been challenging, they say, but rewarding in its own ways.

"Engineering pays a lot better, I'll tell you that," Van Riper says. "So until the salary catches up there's always that. But, you know, it's nice to have your own business and your own equity in it."

But can this type of small, local brewing model truly scale beyond the taproom and limited distribution to become a sustaining, growing business? It can, if the circumstances are right, and Kevin DeLange with Dry Dock Brewing Company in Aurora, Colorado, knows all about it.

He started his company in 2005 with Michelle Reding, his now ex-wife. There were only about eighty breweries in the state at the time, and DeLange says that they considered themselves part of the "new wave" of brewery openings just taking off about a decade ago.

Now Dry Dock operates three brewing facilities—two taprooms and a thirty thousand square foot production facility north of Denver International Airport—and is classified as a regional brewery, meaning it produces more than fifteen thousand barrels of beer per year. It's still only distributed in Colorado, though, which is something that DeLange considers a point of pride, given that most other breweries of his size need to be in at least five or six other states to support their sales volumes. His largest production facility was added in 2013 with the support of a $4 million loan—roughly half for the building and half for the equipment and installation—and for the first time, Dry Dock's beers were available via distributor. As recently as 2011, when the brewery started self-distributing its beers, it was only packaging in twenty-two-ounce, large format bottles and working with a sales staff of two. They quickly realized they couldn't keep up with demand, and the expansion process began almost immediately.

It didn't start out like this, though.

Dry Dock Brewing began as a side business that DeLange and Reding operated out of their homebrew shop, The Brew Hut, which is still in business and located next door to the main taproom in Aurora.

"So we bought the homebrew shop in 2002," DeLange told me one day over beers at his bustling taproom, "and the guy I bought from said, 'if I didn't find a buyer, I was going to do a manufacturing brewery with a manufacturing license, so you don't have to do food and you can sell your own beer for consumption on premises.' And that idea kind of stuck with me for a few years. Then this space became available next door and I called the state and said, 'Hey, can I do this?' and they said, 'Yes, you can.' So we started brewing our own stuff right here in the shop."

They started with a seven-barrel system, essentially brewing for themselves and their limited customer base, but it was a time of great experimentation in terms of recipes, DeLange says, because at least once a week his homebrew customers were bringing in their beers for him to sample. It was an education in what different yeasts and malts and hops can do for the final flavor of a given beer. And, by selling the raw ingredients for so long and being part of an active homebrewing community, he learned all about the various options available and how to source what he needed to make the beers he liked.

"Even today I can still, if I want develop a recipe, I can say, 'I want a really light, American pale ale that doesn't have a lot of hop bitters but it's really dry and it's not very sweet,' and I can sit down and just write a recipe. I know what goes into it. But making it the same each time? I could do that if I wanted to, I just don't have that technical side, but the homebrew shop really helped with the recipe development side for sure."

These days, his brewing staff works on a forty-barrel system at their production facility, capable of doing 120,000 barrels per year when starting new batches every two hours. It's a four-vessel system, so new batches can start once the process is about halfway through.

So how did he do it?

Dry Dock was well positioned—and well timed—to take advantage of the growing market for craft beer in 2010–2011, but DeLange explains his growth philosophy has always been a series of baby steps. Three years after they bought the homebrew shop, they started brewing their own beers on a commercial basis. Two years later, they added a new, expanded brewhouse and then expanded their taproom. And two years after that, they went all-in on their thirty-thousand-square-foot brewing facility and added distribution. Every step was stressful, he says, but they knew that it would always be better to wait another year, find a little extra capital to get into the right building, and install the bigger system, rather than continually have to upgrade as they grew.

And, full disclosure: funding this process was a little easier for them than it would be for new brewers today, in part because lenders have soured on breweries as a business model due to overcrowding in the market. Turns out, getting started at the beginning of the second craft beer boom was a good move for Dry Dock. Had DeLange and Reding waited just a few years, they likely wouldn't have been able to get ahead of the crowds storming into the industry and would have faced significant headwinds.

"The biggest thing for us to begin with was making the best brew we can and then figuring out how to sell it. When we talk about what we're going to make and getting into the quality of the ingredients, the big thing is, and this is still the case, that the brewers can buy whatever ingredients they need to make the best beer they can make. We'll see if we can make money on it afterward."

CHAPTER 7

INGREDIENTS

"[Brewing beer] really isn't any harder than baking a batch of cookies. What is difficult is understanding how to make cookies when you have never seen it done before."

—John Palmer, author, *How to Brew:*
Everything You Need to Know to Brew Beer Right the First Time

*T*he retrofitted grain elevator that Grouse Malting and Roasting Company calls home is of the traditional "wood-cribbed" design, popular throughout the United States in the early twentieth century, with a metal or clapboard skin built around a wood beam frame. Structures of this type have since been replaced by steel and concrete silos for commercial use, due to the risk of fire in a wood-framed building, but the general function has changed very little throughout the decades. A bucket elevator is used to lift grain to a distribution point at the top of the building where it is dumped through a series of spouts that direct it, using gravity, to different parts of the building, either for storage or for transport. Emptying out the final product follows a similar path, using gravity to drain the silos or bins into rail cars, trucks, bags, or other means for transport to flour mills, breweries, ethanol producers, and other processing destinations. This was not only an important function in early American farming, before the use of powered tools, but also through more recent years in the rural West, where access to power was not always reliable or economical. A gravity-driven system just works, no matter what.

In Grouse Malting's case, its metal-skinned elevator in Wellington, Colorado, no longer functions as a true storage space (they aren't doing the kind of volume yet that calls for processing silos worth of raw materials), but the building does serve as a nice conversation piece and functional processing space for the craft malting company.

"Five years ago when we moved in, this was a dump," Will Soles, the company's special projects manager, carpenter, equipment, and facility manager, and all around go-to guy (he's described as MacGyver-like by his boss), tells me as we walk through the converted, three-thousand-square-foot space. He points out the corner where the musty old carpets had been rolled up, where the rusty welding debris had been stored, and even where some of the water stains on the ceiling had been. The building had been vacant for a number of years before Grouse leased it. "We redid everything. Wiped the floors, put paint on the walls, cleaned everything, and tried to make it into a nice office."

Wellington is a dry and dusty farming town about ten minutes north of Fort Collins and not far from the Colorado-Wyoming border. The downtown area, as it is, stretches for about six blocks along Main Street between the interstate and the open plains with a mix of retail shops, gas stations, bars, and the kind of casual restaurants you'll find in farm towns across the country, all serving up Tex-Mex specials, coffee for a dime all day, and all-you-can-eat breakfast. It's quiet and all but deserted on a Thursday afternoon, with only a few cars rolling through town.

The central part of the firm's grain elevator still shows the wood beams that make up the walls, and the system still works, should the company's owners decide they ever want to use it that way again. ("See, this still goes all the way up to the top.") That's unlikely, however; when I visited, a new brewer was set to take over part of the space for use as a taproom.

When company founder Twila Henley moved the company into this existing location, she converted a one-metric-ton dairy tank into the basic equipment she needed and built a food-grade, climate-controlled space in the middle of the warehouse so she could floor-germinate her malts in larger batches. The grains are roasted outside.

Although "craft malting" is something of a new category in the food production world, the controlled malting process has, literally, been around for thousands of years, a key part of humankind's progress from hunter-gatherers to food cultivators. It's a three-step process—steeping, germination, and drying—that remains virtually unchanged from the earliest days of agriculture, and is fairly consistent from malter to malter even today. Craft malt by definition can be produced from barley, wheat, rye, millet, oats, corn, spelt, triticale, and other grains, but always needs to be made using 50 percent or more by weight of locally-grown grains to retain the local flavors of the seed varieties. It also needs to be produced without any chemical additives. The only variance Grouse introduces to the process is its use of gluten-free millet in its base malt products rather than the traditional beer base of barley or wheat, allowing them to sell ingredients for naturally gluten-free beers, a growing niche in craft beer.

Malt itself is nothing more than grain that has been allowed to germinate, or begin growing into a plant, and then stopped before the process goes too far. This releases the enzymes in the seed and opens up the sugars that will eventually be fermented into beer in the wort. By partially germinating the seed, malting effectively breaks free the various resources contained in the barley (or in this case, millet) and presents them in a format that the brewer can use in their recipes.

At Grouse, the raw seed is first sorted when it arrives at the facility, and then it's transferred into a malt vessel where water is added. This steeping starts the germination process by providing "the medium for the biochemical reactions which take place inside the seed kernel." This part of the malting process goes on for about two days, during which time the seed is stirred by hand repeatedly so that it spends time both submerged and uncovered, allowing the grain time to rest and introducing oxygen into the process. Once the seed has absorbed enough moisture to allow for the uniform breakdown of its starches and proteins, it will begin to show what Henley refers to as "chit," or early-stage roots visibly poking out the side of the kernel.

From there, the grain is toted via bucket elevator from the steeping tank to the germination room to continue the modification stage that will break down the seed's starch reserves, resulting in fermentable sugars. Spread evenly across the food-safe floor in this dark, humid, twenty by twenty–foot room, the grain truly becomes malt. It doesn't happen automatically, though. Malters have to periodically turn the grain to keep the grain bed from overheating and the rootlets from growing together, a natural process known as felting that helps plants in the wild survive. Large commercial malting operations have automated rakes and shovels that perform this task for them, but at Grouse, someone has to go into the germination room in person every four to eight hours, twenty-four hours a day, and shovel the grain by hand.

"We try to keep as high a moisture level in the room as possible," Soles tells me as we peer into the dark, low-ceilinged space. "That way the grain doesn't dry out. And then we usually keep it right around 70 degrees in there, too, so it doesn't get too hot."

This is where timing comes in, as well as the malter's understanding of the natural forces at play. If the grain were left to germinate for longer than about three days, the kernel would continue to grow and would eventually become a full plant. This would be fine for the grain, but it would use up all of the starch reserves the brewer is counting on to make their beer, rendering the malt useless for brewing purposes. That's why germination is halted midway through the process by kiln-drying the grain until it reaches a shelf-stable moisture content. The time and temperature involved vary from product to product—some specialty malts are treated in the kiln for longer or shorter periods or at different temperatures to bring out specific roasting characteristics, like color and flavor—but on average, the drying process for standard barley- or millet-base malt takes about a day. The final malt is then cleaned and deculmed, which removes the germinated rootlets from the grains, as those roots can impart unwanted bitterness to beer.

Grouse can do three malt-production cycles per week, given its current equipment setup, and the whole process takes six days from start to finish.

Oddly enough, the term *maltster*, or *maltstress*, in this case, is not common, even in the world of craft malting and brewing, but Grouse Malting founder, CEO, and maltstress (it's on her business cards), Twila Henley is committed to bringing it back.

And she has the résumé to back it up, starting with an undergraduate degree in nutrition from Miami University in Ohio and a master's in food science and food safety from Colorado State University. Her graduate studies focused on malting and brewing science as well as bioactive and probiotic compounds, and she started Grouse as a side project in 2010, only moving it to a full-time business in 2013. She is a founding board member of the North American Craft Maltster's Guild and remains one of just a handful of full-time, craft malters in the United States.

But craft malting is a niche within a niche, she admits, even as the brewing industry has taken off in recent years. Corporate macrobrewers like MillerCoors and Anheuser-Busch generally contract with large malt producers to supply their base ingredients, and even craft brewers today simply need more malt than small operators like Grouse can provide. In fact, the world of malt generally boils down to fewer than a dozen national suppliers, and the market for brewers looking for small orders of local, craft-made malt are few and far between. Still, Henley is not deterred.

"One thing that I was really struck with when I moved to Colorado and I started to see what was going on with this craft brewing scene was I just couldn't believe the black curtain that covered up ingredients," she says. "There was a lot of push about local beer and how great this all is, but you really didn't have to dig too far to be like, wait a second—it's great that I'm supporting my local homebrewer but where are they getting their ingredients? Where is the malt coming from?"

She soon discovered that most brewers still get their base malt from just a few producers in this country and overseas. Craft malting, in which the producer can control not only the quality and source of the grains going into the malt, but also the flavor profile that comes out on the other side, was just starting to gain steam among small commercial brewers and homebrew enthusiasts. As of 2013, only twenty craft maltsters operated in North America, ranging from Maltarie Frontenac in Quebec, Canada, the largest at 400 tons of annual capacity, to Our Mutual Friend Malt & Brew in Denver, which produces only as much malt as it needs to brew the beer for its taproom. Of these, a few are clustered in New York, Colorado, and Oregon, with the rest scattered across the country. And that's pretty much it for domestic brewing malts at the craft level.

It wasn't always this way. According to the North American Craft Malting Guild, prior to prohibition in the 1930s, malthouses could be found all over the United States, particularly in the Midwest where the grain supplies were plentiful. Obviously, when many American breweries were forced to close as a result of the outlaw legislation, many of these small independent malters struggled to find new customers and the vast majority went out of business. The few houses that survived this period emerged with a near monopoly on the industry (much like the brewers that survived that period) that, in many ways, persists to this day.

"Today, the majority of malt is produced by only a handful of companies," the Craft Malting Guild writes, "but because of the growing popularity of micro and craft-brewing and desire for local ingredients, small scale malt houses are reemerging. This monopolization of the malting industry is very similar to that of the brewing industry before the micro or craft-brewing boom in the 1980s."

Henley's office in the Grouse grain elevator is spacious and wood-paneled, clean and tidy considering it sits about fifty feet from an operating production floor. Crafts and assorted art projects line the walls, giving the room the feel of a middle school guidance counselor's office. We sit at an octagonal oak farmhouse table, which does double-duty as Grouse Malting's conference table.

The pivot for Henley, from craft malter to gluten-free craft malter, came in 2008, when she was diagnosed with ulcerative colitis, an autoimmune disease similar to Crohn's and celiac disease. It triggers an immune response in the digestive system that leads to all sorts of unpleasant symptoms, and she soon found that following a gluten-free diet helped ease her symptoms. As an enthusiastic beer drinker, however, she was less than impressed with the available gluten-free options at the time, and her journey into gluten-free malting began.

"Is it too much to ask for a delicious gluten-free beer?" she writes on the Grouse Malting website. "The idea was challenging, and it became a personal goal to create an awesome tasting beer that just happens to also be gluten-free."

The project began as a partnership with a local millet farmer. As it turns out, the state of Colorado is the largest millet producer in the United States, and most of that millet has traditionally been used in birdseed. The increasing popularity of gluten-free foods, however, has brought new attention to humble millet grain, which cooks up to a consistency that's much like quinoa and is naturally gluten free. It also doesn't contain many allergens, according to Henley, and is considered a staple in parts of Africa. When used to brew beer, millet grains produce a gluten-free brew that sacrifices next to nothing in terms of flavor or mouthfeel.

And, if Grouse's experience is any guide, it's taking hold in the brewing community.

"We actually sell coast-to-coast," Henley says, "which is definitely different [from some of the other craft malters]. Craft malting is all about locality and tying the local farmer to the local brewer. We definitely have an aspect of that, but it's not the biggest value-add that we bring to the table, because we do have customers elsewhere getting our products."

It all starts with the ingredients.

The basic process of brewing beer, as mentioned earlier, is fairly straightforward. Malted barley is boiled in water to release its fermentable sugars, the resulting sugar liquid is boiled with hops and other additives for seasoning and preservation purposes, yeast is added to the mix to begin the fermentation process, and after a few weeks, the final beer is bottled with a bit of extra sugar to create carbonation. That's pretty much all there is to it, and it doesn't vary too much whether you're creating a five-gallon batch in your kitchen or a hundred barrels at a time at a commercial brewery.

"To learn to brew beer, you don't need to learn how the yeast metabolizes the malt sugars, but you do need to understand that eating sugar is what they do," writes John Palmer in *How to Brew*, "and you need to understand what they need from you to get the job done. Once you understand that, you can do your part, they can do theirs, and good beer will happen."

Whether they understand the science behind it, for small craft brewers and nanobrewing operations, the question of ingredients can be a crucial. Not only will their choices contribute to the flavor and quality of their end products, but they also often play into their business identity. Maybe they want to focus on local suppliers to differentiate themselves from the competition, sourcing their malts and hops and other ingredients from the surrounding area. Or maybe they prefer to use specialized components, such as Grouse Malting's gluten-free malt or specialty hops that other brewers aren't using, to make their products more unique. Either way, the choice of what a brewer puts into their beer is key in the craft market, as it often affects both their flavors and their sales pitches.

Ryan Skeels and Kevin Greer, the co-owners of Baere Brewing Company in Denver, are in the former camp and choose to go local with their ingredients both to highlight the quality of Colorado's ingredients and to support their fellow small business owners. They buy their yeast, for instance, from a small, two-man shop in Arvada, Colorado, and get their malts and grains from a supplier located on the state's Eastern Plains.

"They just deliver right to your door," Skeels says of their yeast supplier, "and they're cheaper than other people. If you want something different, they'll talk to you. They can try to get what you want."

The growth of the craft beer industry in the United States is well known at this point, but what's not as well known is the growth of associated companies like ingredient suppliers, equipment makers, brewing technology developers, and others alongside it. These are the folks who truly make craft beer work from behind the scenes, and many insiders expect to see a wave of new auxiliary companies like these emerging over the next few years.

Part of this is thanks to the larger players in the craft brewing movement. With the success of brewers like New Belgium, Sierra Nevada, and Brooklyn Brewing, all of which are calling on suppliers for literal tons of malt and other components every month, a steady demand now exists in the market to support these craft ingredients. That means it now makes more economic sense for suppliers and distributors to grow and stock the more unique products that smaller brewers need and at prices they can afford. For instance, if a malt production house is able to count on a $25,000 standing monthly order from one of the major craft brewers, it won't have to worry about keeping the lights on as much as it would if it were relying solely on one-off $500 sales. As a result, it may be better able to sell its extra malt off to those homebrewers and small-timers. Or maybe it can find room in its malting schedule to produce the specialty malt that some of its smaller customers are asking for. Either way, a healthy market for malt helps producers and brewers at all levels.

The same goes for specialty hops, yeasts, brewing equipment, and staff. When the overall industry is healthy and growing, the success of the brewers at the top trickles down to the local players in the form of ingredients, know-how, and economies of scale.

And, as with any instance of supply and demand, the suppliers are starting to see the growing market for craft brewing ingredients and are expanding to serve the need, opening up operations in busy brewing locations like Portland, Oregon; Asheville, North Carolina; and Boulder, Colorado. Some of these are new additions to the market, and some are outposts of more established firms. (For example, one of the leading yeast suppliers in the country, White Labs, has offices in San Diego, California; Davis, California; Boulder; Asheville; Chicago, Illinois; and even Copenhagen, Denmark, to serve local brewers in those areas.) In addition to supplying the unique products nanobrewers need at their scale, these local operations are also able to offer better customer service, faster turnaround, and higher-quality ingredients across the board.

"I think before a few years ago, there wasn't a yeast company even east of us; everything was out west," Greer says. "Now there's a bunch of companies popping up on the East Coast that are doing cool stuff. And since America's obsessed with sours, some of the companies are doing really cool sour blends and stuff that they're real proud of."

Skeels agrees: "They've embraced the craft mentality. Just being cool with everybody, and focusing on being local."

As it happens, ingredients are one area where small brewers are at an advantage versus their larger competition. Due to the simple math involved—a five-barrel batch of beer requires fewer raw ingredients than a fifteen-barrel batch does—nanobrewers are better able not only to roll with the punches and adjust their recipes based on available ingredients, but they also don't have to look very far to get the pieces they need for a particular brew.

For example, Craig Rothgery with the tiny De Steeg Brewing credits his small size for helping keep him nimble in the market. He had been in business for just over two years when I met with him in early 2015. Brewing on a small system, he says, has made it possible to get to more than one hundred different beers in just over two years by keeping his ingredient costs down and minimizing the amounts required for each batch.

"That's the great part of being a small brewery," he says. "I can go to a homebrew shop and buy ingredients if I need to; we're small enough for that."

Even if he runs out of something on the day of the brew, Rothgery says he's not above making a run to the grocery store to pick up what he needs. Obviously, few typical neighborhood stores carry things like base malt, hop pellets, or brewers yeast, but for flavoring agents, fruit add-ins, or other spices in limited quantities, they work in a pinch, especially since he isn't buying too much at a time. Of course, that all goes out the window once a brewer starts working on a ten- or fifteen-barrel system; at that level, they would need more of a particular ingredient than most grocery stores would typically carry, making the sort of roll-with-the-punches, go-with-what's-available flexibility that Rothgery enjoys that much more difficult.

The trick for any brewer, he admits, is finding reproducible ingredients. Think about it; let's say you go to the market to buy oranges for your citrus-flavored wheat beer. Okay, that's great. But are the oranges you buy a week later for the next batch going to taste the same? Will they even taste the same the next day, let alone sixth months from now? It's hard to say, and even the grocer or farmer can't be sure, so that's why many brewers have a hard time trying to reproduce specific flavors at scale, and why consistent, baseline ingredients (like pasteurized orange juice instead of the real thing) can sometimes become necessary as batch sizes go up. Nature can be, to put it mildly, occasionally inconsistent.

"When I worked in food processing, it was all about how do you get reproducible ingredients?" Rothgery says. "Okay, we want to make this product but this is all of the ingredient that we need that we can get from our supplier right now. What do we do? And when you're baking thousands, and thousands, and thousands of pounds of stuff, that's really important. People might think, 'how about you throw this in there?' but it's not that easy, you know."

But, even given all the advantages that come with brewing on a small system, that's not to say that nanobrewers don't face other ingredient-related challenges even at their limited scale. Without access to some of the sourcing channels that the larger players rely on, sometimes they have to get creative. Rothgery recently made a fifteen-barrel batch of ginger ale on a friend's system and ended up having to special order thirty-five pounds of fresh ginger from the Sprouts Farmers' Market in his neighborhood. That solution worked for his purposes, but for any brewer working on a larger scale, having those ingredient channels in place ahead of time is far more important and helps cut down on production costs.

"Like just trying to keep up with guys like me," he says. "If I want to brew something interesting, I can go to the store tomorrow and brew it the next day. For the bigger guys, there's a lot more planning, there's a lot more tests. God forbid you go brew a gigantic 120-barrel batch of something and it turns out bad. I have a lot less that I'm risking by brewing an experimental batch. It's much easier to be flexible at this scale than at the larger scale."

Even slightly larger craft brewers are at a disadvantage in this way when compared to Rothgery's one-barrel system. "I put out a new beer every two weeks. That is not something most people can do. That's the nice part about being small."

When it comes to assembling the various "parts" of a recipe into a final beer, flavor and style are not truly as simple as just choosing the "right" ingredients, mixing them together, and hoping for the best. Given the fairly short ingredient list that goes into your typical beer, craft or not, each of those few ingredients tends to loom large in the flavor department by the time the brewer reaches the final product.

Take the malt, for instance. The total grain bill for a brewing recipe most often consists of a combination of different malted grains, each bringing their own characteristics to the mix. It can be produced using any cereal grain, as proven by the gluten-free products being produced by Grouse Malting, but most base malts for brewing are made from two primary varieties of barley: two-row and six-row. The all-around, most common choice is two-row, with six-row more often used in lighter lagers and ales. Specialty malts are also made from two-row and six-row barley, as well as other grains—including wheat, rye, spelt, rice, and corn—that have been kiln-dried or processed differently than base malts to bring out diverse colors and flavors.

"What do Whoppers, Long John Silver's, Ovaltine, and beer all have in common?" ask authors Christina Perozzi and Hallie Beaune in their 2009 book, *The Naked Pint: An Unadulterated Guide to Craft Beer.* "Well, those chocolate-covered candies, the vinegar you sprinkle on your fish and chips, and that powder you stir into your milk are made with malt, which just happens to be the basis for all the color, alcohol content, viscosity, carbonation, and subsequent mouthfeel of beer. . . . The color to which the malt has been roasted (and the combination of the colors of malt) is solely responsible for the color of that beer. The amount of malt used, in conjunction with the amount of yeast used, is solely responsible for the alcohol content and carbonation of that beer."

Malt Varieties

The grain options in brewing break down roughly as follows:

Base Malt: This is where it all starts, accounting for the majority of the malt in most recipes and providing "most of the enzymatic (diastatic) power to convert starches into fermentable sugars," according to *BeerAdvocate*. As the name implies, the base malts form the grain "base" of the recipe, providing not only most of the sugar and starch extract potential for the mash, but also the primary flavor and mouthfeel characteristics. On top of this, the brewer will add roasted, flavored, and other specialty malts, depending on the style of beer they want to brew, with any given recipe including five or more different styles of malt.

Light: Specialty malts that have been kiln-dried at higher temperatures than those used for base malts are classified as "light," although they are often deeper in color than most base malt grains and bring a fuller, stronger malt flavor to the final beer. Due to the higher heat used in the drying process, light malts offer less enzymatic activity and cannot be used on their own in place of base malt (which is a common characteristic of all roasted specialty malts) as they do not release the same amount of sugars to the mash. But when mixed with traditional base malts, they bring their own flavor characteristics to the table. Pale ale and lager malts, are both classified as light malts, as are Vienna and Munich malts, both of which are commonly used in German lager-style beers.

Dark: As the name implies, dark specialty malts are kiln-dried at even higher temperatures and for longer durations than light malts, resulting in darker colors and stronger flavors that lend themselves to styles such as stouts and porters.

The roasting process, however, effectively ends all enzyme activity for these malts, meaning that dark malts are only used for color and flavor and do not contribute any fermentable sugars to the mash.

Caramel: Unlike light and dark malts simply roasted after drying for flavoring, so-called caramel malts are dried more slowly to bring out the natural sugars in the barley. These malts are roasted at a set temperature over a longer period of time to caramelize the malt, just as the sugars in onions and other vegetables are said to carmelize when heated slowly in a pan. The end result is a malt ranging in color from light to dark amber with a flavor profile focused on mild sweetness, malty mouthfeel, and burned sugar undertones.

Wheat: One exception to the rule of a base malt bill being combined with one or more specialty malts is found in the wheat-style beers, which are typically made with 100 percent wheat as their bases. Given that it's a more gluten-heavy malt bill than typical barley malt, the use of wheat gives the final beer a hazy appearance, but the proteins in the grain contribute to a richer mouthfeel, fuller body, and better head stability. For this reason, wheat is sometimes used in partnership with barley malts in non-wheat beer styles to bring out these characteristics.

Adjuncts: The list of "other" grains and flavoring agents that can be added to the malt bill in beer recipes is long and varied, including everything from unmalted cereal grains like rye, to corn grits, rice, oats, and more. These adjuncts help reduce the cost of the brew by cutting the amount of more expensive barley ingredients needed for the mash, but also often bring other characteristics to the final beer in their own right, including new flavors, better mouthfeel, and stronger foam retention. For example, corn is the most popular adjunct in American breweries (particularly at the macro, corporate level) both because it contributes a mild sweet flavor to the beer and can help lighten the overall body and haze of the final product. What's more, corn is widely available in the United States, generally consistent in terms of quality, and very cheap. Rice, the second-most used adjunct in the United States, on the other hand, contributes almost nothing in terms of flavor so it allows the natural characteristics of the other malts to shine through. Beers brewed with rice as an adjunct, of which

Budweiser is probably the best known, tend to be dry and crisp, which can be a desirable characteristic depending on the beer style.

And that's just the malts. Hops take everything a step further, with more than one hundred different types and styles in wide use, each with their own flavor and brewing characteristics.

Hops, as most of us know them, are the female, flowering buds of the *humulus lupulus* plant, a perennial plant often farmed vertically as climbing bines (a "bine" is any plant that climbs by growing around a support line, rather than by using suckers as vines do) that can reach twenty feet high. As a perennial plant, hops are essentially a weed that growers simply train to climb up wires or strings during the growing season each year, harvesting the final crop in the fall. At full height, they look something like grape plants in a vineyard, albeit much taller, with wide flat leaves and, in place of grape bunches, small pinecone-like hop buds that contain the bittering oils the brewers need.

In beer, hops serve as both flavoring and stability agents, by adding both their trademark bitter flavor the final brew and serving an antibacterial function that helps the brewer's yeast prevail over less desirable wild yeasts during the brewing process. These additives also help prevent spoilage during fermentation, contribute to head retention, and help make for a crisp, clear beer.

Brewers as far back as the Middle Ages knew of the preservative properties of hops—the first recorded use of hops in beer was by Benedictine abbess and writer Hildegard of Bingen in the twelfth century—and appreciated the ingredient for its potential to improve the flavor of their then thin, low-alcohol beers. The use of hops eventually replaced the other bittering agents that brewers had been using until that point, including dandelion flowers, burdock root, marigold, ivy, and heather. Cultivation of the plant, which began in central Europe, soon spread to all of the major brewing regions of the world, and hops soon became an essential ingredient in modern beer.

"Hops are a natural preservative, and part of the early use of hops in beer was to help preserve it," writes Palmer in *How to Brew*. "This is how one particular style of beer, India pale ale, was developed. At the turn of the 18th century, British brewers began shipping strong ale with lots of hops added to the barrels to preserve it during the several-month voyage to India. By journey's end, the beer had acquired a depth of hop aroma and flavor—perfect for quenching the thirst of British personnel in the tropics."

Perozzi and Beaune take a somewhat lighter approach in their own description of the importance of hops to the brewing process:

"We like to use the analogy that malts are the male part of beer," they write. "You have to encourage them to grow; you have to cajole, manipulate, and control them to make them useful. Hops are the female part of beer. They come in many varieties and can easily dominate, can be quite flowery, can be high maintenance, and are often bitter. (Just kidding . . . kind of.)"

Hop Varieties

The list of hop varieties is far too long to examine fully here (and that's to say effectively nothing about the "noble hops," the four primary hop varieties in traditional European brewing—Tettnanger, Spalt, Hallertauer, and Saaz—known for their low bitterness levels and high aromas, which are perfect for German pilsners and similar styles), but the list dates roughly back to 1919 when Professor E. S. Salmon in Kent, England, became the first person to cultivate specific types of hop when he introduced both the Brewer's Gold and Bullion varieties. As of 2015, more than eighty different hops are used in brewing, but some of the most popular, widely-used types of hops are:

Cascade: One of the oldest and most popular hop varieties in American craft brewing, Cascade hops come with a backstory. The variety, the first of the "Three Cs" of American hops, was first developed in the late 1950s as part of Oregon State University's breeding program and officially released for use in the early 1970s. Featuring a spicy, flowery flavor with undertones of citrus and grapefruit, Cascade hops were first used commercially by the New Albion Brewing Company in Sonoma, California (a.k.a. the first American craft brewery) in its category-defining pale ale and have since become all but synonymous with American ales.

Centennial: The second of the "Three Cs" of American hops, Centennial hops have been in use since 1990, having been bred as a hybrid of several different European styles. Centennial hops bring strong citrus aromas similar in style to Cascade hops but stepped up a notch in terms of overall intensity.

Citra: Introduced in 2007 and heavy on the citrus fruit and tropical aromas, the name Citra is a registered trademark of the Hop Breeding Company. Citras are among the more popular hops in use today and appear in many nano and craft brewed pale ales and IPAs.

Chinook: A hybrid of two different hop varieties from the Washington-Idaho region, Chinook hops have been used in brewing since 1985 and are considered one of the "trademark" hop varieties of Pacific Northwest–style brewing, adding a slightly spicy flavor with heavy pine and evergreen overtones.

Columbus: The third and final of the "Three Cs" on this list, Columbus hops are very heavy on the citrus flavors and bitterness, like Cascades and Centennials, but add a dose of extra oil to the mix, resulting in what brewers describe as a very "resiny" feel to the final beer.

Fuggle: Not an American hop variety, but rather an English strain that led to many American offshoots grown today in the Pacific Northwest, Fuggle hops can be traced back to a strain of wild (i.e., uncultivated) hops that was discovered in the southeastern corner of the United Kingdom in the 1860s. By the 1950s, nearly 80 percent of the entire English crop of hops comprised Fuggle hops. A fairly mild hop when compared to many of the American varieties, Fuggles are generally used as aroma hops and contribute very mild bitterness, which lends itself very well to many English-style ales. The US Fuggle is a domestic offshoot that is milder still than true English Fuggles but adds a woodsy aroma and well-rounded character to the style.

Galena: The most widely-grown American hop variety, Galena hops have been in use since 1978 and originated as part of an open pollination breeding involving the Brewers Gold variety and an unknown second plant. With a mild, well-balanced bitterness similar to Chinooks but dialed back a notch, Galenas are popular for use in lagers, ales, and other styles as a general purpose bittering agent that doesn't overpower the other ingredients, as other American hops can.

Golding: Another English hop with a long history, the mild Golding hop has been popular in English brewing since the eighteenth century. Today, a number of different "sub Goldings" are available, such as Kent Goldings and Pethams, depending on where they are grown, as well as US-grown versions based on the Canterbury style. They all share a similar smooth flavor, though, with spicy aromas that pair well with classic English-style ales.

Mount Hood: Named for Mount Hood in Oregon, this variety was cultivated in 1983 and features a spicy aroma and clean, bitter taste. It's considered one of the "softer" American varieties and its clean flavor is popular in German and American lagers as well as other styles that need bitterness without much hop aroma.

Willamette: Another Pacific Northwest hop that's named for its home region—in this case, the Willamette Valley in Oregon—Willamette hops are a variation on the Fuggle hop variety and have been in use since the 1970s. Highly fragrant, spicy, and woodsy, Willamettes are very popular in American brewing, making up nearly 20 percent of the total US crop.

No matter what the variety, though, hops themselves are traditionally grown vertically on long cords, rising up in tidy rows that reach far overhead, thick and green as trees by the time they're ready to harvest. In the United States, the height of these trellises is roughly standardized at eighteen feet—in large part because much of the equipment used to harvest hops is built with this height in mind—though there is some variety from region to region. Along Colorado's Front Range, for example, where hop farms are far less plentiful than they are in the Pacific Northwest, some early growers started out using twelve-foot trellises to make their own harvests more manageable and to keep the plants from getting overly unwieldy in the area's high winds. That hurt their overall yields, though, and after a few years, just about every hop farmer in the region had switched to the industry standard eighteen-foot trellis. (Those early comers are easy to spot these days, too. All you have to do is drive around northern Colorado in the spring, before the lines go up, and look for the hop trellises that have six-foot extensions nailed onto them.)

At Ron and Michelle Yovich's Ella J Farms near Longmont, Colorado, their hops grow on lines made from coconut shells and are strung by hand, generally by a crew of friends and family, every May. At harvest, these lines are cut down right along with the hop vines themselves and fed straight into a sorting machine that removes the hop cones from the plants and discards the vines, leaves, and lines as one unit. Since the cords are plant matter themselves, Yovich is able to grind up all of this excess material and use it to fertilize his farm for the next season.

"What you're seeing in this section right here are the Cascades and the Chinooks," Ron's brother, Rob, who works full time as the manager of a Motel 6 in Wyoming and helps out at the farm occasionally on his time off, tells me as we walk along the rows. "They're the most popular and the ones that get used a lot. The Mount Hoods like these here are also fairly popular, especially as you get over into the western states, the West Coast states."

Rob, along with Ron's father-in-law, Morie Block, who spent his career in the Pacific Northwest before retiring to Colorado, were at the ten-acre Ella J Farms setting up the lines for that year's hop crop when I visited in spring of

2015. The stringing process takes about three weeks and generally requires at least eight or ten people working full time to do it right. That can be tough to accomplish, though, Ron tells me later, in part because finding temporary labor of this type in this area isn't easy.

"Hops aren't very labor intensive overall," he says, "but they are very, very labor intensive for certain parts of the year," primarily during the stringing and again during the harvest. "But once [the stringing is] done, you don't need them for the rest of the summer. And then harvest time you need them back for about three weeks at the end of August into September."

In hop-growing regions like the Pacific Northwest, a whole system is in place to keep workers busy throughout the growing season. The same laborers who come to help the hop growers set up their lines in the spring are able, once that work is done, to transition over to working in the local peach and apple orchards, trimming trees, and doing other work through the summer. Then, when harvest season rolls around in the fall, they do the rounds again, harvesting hops in September and then grapes in the nearby vineyards in October. So they're able to get a full season, if not a full year's worth, of work in one place by moving between farms and projects. That type of shared labor system doesn't exist yet in places like Colorado.

It's no accident that most US hops are grown in the Pacific Northwest. According to the Hop Growers of America, which is based in the tiny town of Moxee in south central Washington state, hop growing in the region dates back to the late nineteenth century when early European settlers to the area brought the crop with them. Those early years set the groundwork for what has become the major center for North American hop production, with the state of Washington responsible for more than 70 percent of the continent's hop plantings as of 2015, accounting for some 32,000 acres. Oregon comes in at number two with 6,800 acres, accounting for 15 percent of the annual harvest, according to the Association, followed by Idaho at 4,900 acres and "other states" accounting for 2.7 percent of the overall crop. Canada grows hops on just 257 acres. This jives with the fact that most commercial hop production worldwide happens between 35 and 55 degrees latitude, due to the importance of day length during the growing season and the impact that sunlight exposure has on overall yield.

"So that machine right there, that's what they go through to strip off the buds," Morie points out. At the time of my visit, the farm was still little more than an open field. The hop plants themselves were already there, of course, but were bunched down near the ground like ivy and had yet to begin climbing. "Have you ever seen old farming equipment, like an old thrasher? That's what it looks like. It's stationary, and most of them are, although they're making some new varieties of equipment that can move up and down the field. But the biggest problem is the height, how things are set, for the width of the rows, things like that."

The harvest at Ella J Farm is a fairly manual process, as well. Once the hops—and there are about eleven thousand plants growing on Ella J's ten acres—are ready in the fall, workers come down the rows and cut off each of the strings at the top and bottom, along with the hop plants themselves. Then they haul each plant over to the stripping machine where they're belt-fed, with triangular-shaped metal fingers grabbing the plants and pulling them through, to remove the hop cones from the bines. From there, the hops are dried until they get down to a shelf-stable moisture level of ten percent and are then packaged for shipment. In the case of Ella J, they sell most of their hops to A. C. Golden, which is Coors InBev's in-state craft-style brand that uses only Colorado-grown ingredients in its beer, and the hops are eventually frozen, shipped to Washington state, and pelletized for use in the brewery.

As of 2015, the lack of a pelletizing system in Colorado, or anywhere outside of the Pacific Northwest for that matter, had emerged as a significant bottleneck for the industry (though several small pelletizing operations have started to open up in various hop-growing regions, including near the Yovich farm in Colorado, since then). One in particular is following the same model as Hopunion in Washington, which sells to a lot of the homebrew and small craft brewing markets. In their business model, local hop growers sell their hops to Hopunion, which owns the pelletizer, and then Hopunion turns around and sells the now-pelletized hops under its own brand. It's one way, Yovich says, that small, independent farmers can make good money selling their surplus hops each year, rather than picking and choosing individual brewers who may or may not be in business or ready to pay come harvest time.

"The thing that I always thought was funny is you have to string them clockwise," Rob explains during a break from the work. To reach the tops of the eighteen-foot trellises, they have a scaffold set up in the back of a truck, slowly working their way down the rows as they work. The rows are set ten feet apart and the plants are spaced every three-and-a-half feet in the rows to make this sort of access possible. "Because the plants follow the sun. So as they grow, if you string them the other way, they won't grow up the cord. They're amazing plants."

Michelle had been interested in starting a vineyard to grow grapes for wine, but in Colorado, the best area for grapes is on the Western Slope, several hours away from their home on the Front Range. They considered moving, but scrapped the idea so their kids could finish school in the Longmont area where they lived at the time.

"So we started looking for something else to do on the Front Range here," Ron says. "Basically what we were looking for was something where you could have a high value crop in a small area of land. We didn't have two hundred acres to grow corn or soybeans or sugar beets."

Oddly enough, it was at New Belgium Brewing in nearby Fort Collins where they ran into a student from Colorado State University who was working on a master's thesis about growing hops in Colorado. She explained the growing market for local hops, as well as the fact that Colorado's climate is as well suited to the crop as the Pacific Northwest is, despite the fact that the hop industry was fairly nonexistent in Colorado at the time. Sure, growers in the state had been supplying hops to Coors for years, but many had been driven out of the business in the last few decades thanks to cheaper suppliers from out of state and the uneasy economics of working primarily for one customer all year.

Armed with that information—along with plenty of research into the plant itself and several visits to the existing hop farms on the Western Slope of

Colorado—the Yoviches found their plot of land near Longmont, a one-time sod farm, and decided to give it a go, planting their first hops in 2011.

Still, it's hard work.

"Yeah, ten acres definitely isn't a hobby for hops," he laughs. "I still have a day job that I'm trying to figure out how to weave my way out of. And we have the land there to expand to but we don't have the labor force to do it."

The appeal of local ingredients is not lost on Steve Clark, the co-owner of Troubadour Maltings in Fort Collins. His business partner, Chris Schooley, got his start in food and beverage in the coffee market, sourcing and roasting specialty coffees from around the world, and understands the relationship between small batch ingredients and craft beverages. Since 2014, Troubadour has specialized in roasting locally sourced barley malts for both small and large craft brewing clients in Colorado.

"We have some stuff on tap at Odell the last couple of weeks, which is kind of exciting," Clark says, "so we're really in that kind of stage where we're networking with other brewers and listening to what their needs are. But everybody's super interested in having a malter in town and working with us on specialty malts. Everybody is very much in favor of local, but when push comes to shove, they're probably equally as interested in just having access to something different, something unique [in terms of ingredients]."

It's true. One of the major benefits of working with a local craft malter is the ability to access different types of malts and be able meet the needs of different recipes at a small scale. Most base malts that brewers use in their beers are all fairly similar, using roughly standard barley mixes and resulting in similar flavor characteristics in the final beers. This is good news, because most of the domestic base malt currently being used in American brewing, particularly among craft brewers, is of extremely high quality, with great flavor profiles, resulting in high-quality beers. But it's all (roughly) the same. What about those brewers who want to try something different? Who need something different to stand out in the marketplace? Maybe they are small operators and may not have the scale or reach to differentiate themselves from their competitors through distribution or other more traditional means. Brewing a strange, unusual, or otherwise "different" beer might just be the trick to get noticed. Craft malts can make this possible.

Still, it takes the right type of brewer to be willing to dip their toe into this end of the market, in part because there is some real price sensitivity for nano and startup brewers. Clark is quick to admit that he can't compete on prices compared to what larger, national malt suppliers like Rahr can offer.

"So that's kind of the first hurdle for a lot of the smaller brewers," he says, "but a lot of the smaller breweries are also going into this because they want to have the ability to really kind of play with the malt and have that autonomy. Those are the ones that are very interested in this."

For example, shortly before I met with Clark, he had created a batch of base malt for a local brewer that had quite a bit of red coloring to it. The brewer used it to brew up a single malt beer that was very, very dark without being as heavy as you might expect from a beer that looked like that, and it was due to a base malt that at the time wasn't even commercially available from anyone but Troubadour. A brewer couldn't even order it from a catalog if they wanted to. That's what Clark sees as the big selling point for both local, craft malters like his and the breweries they work with.

"There are a hundred different types of malt out there from different malters that you could buy, all slightly different," he says. "So really what it comes down to for us is the [malting] process has some variability in terms of how long, and at what temperature, and at what humidity, we create the malt. For example, a Munich malt usually is germinated at a slightly higher temperature and at a slightly higher humidity. So there's a whole gamut of possibilities there [as to how the process can be altered to tweak the flavor]."

The next step in the process is to take the germinated grain to the kiln to dry it, which adds several more flavor variables to the process in terms of how long the grain is kiln-dried and at what temperature. That's because, Clark explains, this process of driving the water out of the grain gives the final malt a lot of its character and flavor profile, and ultimately it's the temperature at which the final kiln-drying happens that gives the malt most of its color profile. So, when you combine all of those potential variables, you can get all sorts of different colors and flavors out of the malts, and that's what brewers are particularly interested in.

Even the grains used in the process are fair game.

"Malts can be almost any kind of grain," Clark says, "so we're already seeing people getting some random things to malt and using different types of barley. Even, for example, at Colorado State University. We're working with those guys right now in their wheat lab, and they're giving us a new wheat that they've been working on, a new variety to malt."

Clark says he eventually wants to get into malting rye and other things, including organic grains and other variations. And the business of craft malting isn't just about beer.

"The other aspect is the farming end," he says. "There are so many farmers in Colorado, going back generations, that have grown barley for Coors, but they have also over the years found it not necessarily profitable or Coors may not take it, you know. And then the barley goes into feed and they can't sell it for as much. So we've been able to hand-select some farmers up in northern Colorado who are still very interested in doing this and being a part of the community, but not for Coors, and that's been great."

When I spoke with Clark in 2015, Troubadour had access to about one hundred acres of grain planted across five different farms in Colorado, with plans to ramp up production within the year. Selling it to brewers, he said, was the easy part.

"Literally five miles away is where this was all grown and malted. Who doesn't love that kind of story?

CHAPTER 8

FLAVOR

"God made yeast, as well as dough, and loves fermentation just as dearly as he loves vegetation."

—Ralph Waldo Emerson, poet

To learn more about the microorganism that literally converts the sugars in wort into alcohol—yeast—I paid a visit to Inland Island, a two-man yeast propagation firm located in an industrial park on Denver's north side. Founded in 2014 by a pair of microbiologists who met while working at a biofuels manufacturing company, the company specializes in producing high-quality, individual strain yeasts and blends specifically designed for brewers, with a focus on the homebrew and nanobrewing end of the market.

"It's almost strange to call yeast an ingredient," company cofounder Matthew Peetz told me while pouring what appeared to be four identical pale ales at the facility's small tasting room. "You know, in baking when you think of ingredients you have sugar, flour, or whatever else that you might put in the there. But with many beers, the yeast is actually what is making the alcohol."

Peetz is a cellular biologist by training and has more than five years of full-time yeast experience, including yeast propagation and contamination mitigation skills honed on the commercial level. He and cofounder John Giarratano, a biologist with a background in pharmaceuticals and large-scale process engineering, split off on their own to start Inland Island when they realized there was a huge hole in the market for "craft yeasts." The number of commercial breweries nationwide has been growing exponentially for years, they said, but the industry as a whole continues to buy nearly all of its yeast for all of its beers from four primary suppliers. Brewing Science in Woodland Park, Colorado, has been at it since 1996 and serves a wide variety of clientele, as does Wyeast in Oregon, in business since 1986, while GigaYeast, located south of San Francisco, is a more recent upstart, founded in 2011. But most brewers are familiar with White Labs. Headquartered in San Diego, the company has been a major supplier to the industry on all levels, from homebrewing to large-scale commercial operations.

"There are hundreds of different strains of yeast you can use that are regularly used in breweries, and there are far more in nature," Peetz says. "So it's something that is constantly evolving. So a brewer's choice in what yeast they're going to use a lot of times defines the style of beer that they're going to make, or just what flavor they're going to get out of it."

In the face of this well-established competition, Inland Island has gone for a familiar differentiator in the craft foods and beverage space—offering a local product—and a lot of their business plan mirrors what many nano and craft brewers have been doing for years: buying local.

And, for yeast, this comes with another advantage.

"Yeast is affected by time and traveling and storage," Giarratano explains. "And so by offering the absolute freshest product that we can, I think our product quality is better than anything else offered out there. We're also, because we're kind of catering to these smaller breweries, we're delivering the proper yeast to them so their fermentations work properly, and offering them a much higher level of customer service."

With yeast, freshness is measured in days if not hours—the samples that Peetz and Giarratano grow in their lab double in size every two hours, for example—and full orders take a week or more to fully form and go through testing. It is a very controlled process that takes place in a clean room via a proprietary process the founders developed in an effort to both maximize yeast production and ensure the highest quality strains for their customers.

Still, yeast remains, to many people, brewers included, a bit of a mystery. Yeast isn't the kind of thing that many brewers, especially new commercial brewers, really want to mess around with, because the process is so complex and the price of failure can be so high. A mismeasured yeast pitch or a low-quality strain can be the difference between a successful batch and a very expensive, in terms of both time and ingredient cost, lesson in failed brewing.

The tricky thing about yeast is that it's not technically an ingredient in the brewing process in the same way that hops and malt are ingredients. It's a living thing, an organism that actively contributes to the creation of the alcohol in beer.

But yeast also contributes a great deal in the way of flavor to the final product. No two strains taste the same—Belgian yeasts, for example, are essentially what make Belgian beers "Belgian" by introducing many of the trademark banana and citrus fruit flavors to those recipes—and that twist on the overall flavor profile is something the brewer takes into account when creating their recipes. The United States, oddly, is one of the few places on the planet that likes to create different varieties of beer rather than just focusing on one or two styles, as is common in Europe. Walk into a German brewery, for example, and you won't find three different IPAs, a brown ale, a pale ale, and all the rest on the taproom menu. You'll find their house beer (probably a lager), one or two variations on it, and that will probably be about it. It's done this way because the brewer makes that particular beer really, really well, and a lot of that success is due to the yeast that's used in the process. At many traditional brewhouses, these brewers often have one house yeast that works for what they do that they have been using over and over again (by pulling a bit from each batch they brew) for generations.

"Back in the day, nobody was growing yeast," Peetz explains, "and so the legend was that, like the Vikings when they brewed beer, they had a stick they passed down from father to son and they'd say, 'A long as you stir the sugar water with this stick, it will turn into beer.' And it was because yeast was living on that stick. That's just one form of artificial selection, and obviously when it stops working, you toss that stick. The good sticks stay around, and the good yeasts become more and more available."

This is roughly what happened in English, Belgian, German, and other breweries centuries ago. Most brewers, even those days, were just collecting their yeast every time they brewed beer so they could use it in their next batches. That's how yeasts became "regionalized," according to Peetz. When those early brewers ran out of yeast at their breweries, they would just go get yeast from the next closest brewhouse, just like a neighbor borrowing a cup of sugar, and thereby extending the use of each strain. So it was the geography of Europe, and the fact that all these brewers were working in such close proximity at the same time, that helped create an environment where many English strains of year are related, many Belgian strains are related, and so on down the line.

All of this "domestication" of yeast is a fairly recent phenomenon, beginning only in 1841 when yeasts were discovered to be the driving force behind fermentation. As a result, specific strains were identified and isolated by early chemists and brewers, based primarily on the flavors, textures, and other characteristics they brought to individual beer styles. (This same process happened with other products around this time, as well, as yeast is also fundamental to bread, wine, and more, and certain strains perform better for each application.) As with any type of unnatural selection, this did not happen automatically—yeasts that became identified with these "positive" characteristics were isolated by brewers simply by using them in their recipes over and over again.

All of this happened, quite literally, by accident. The circumstances surrounding the creation of the first fermented beverage have been lost to history (though many experts believe it predated the Ancient Egyptian civilizations that often get credit for "inventing" beer), but it is widely believed to have occurred when some sugary solution was left out too long and wild yeast was allowed to ferment it. Early drinkers enjoyed the results, but it would be thousands of years until the true science behind fermentation was understood and reliably reproducible. Peetz's story earlier about the "magic stick" was the literal truth for many early brewers and winemakers. Without that yeast delivery mechanism, whatever it was, they had no way of knowing if a given batch of beer, wine, or whatever other beverage they were trying to make would ferment. Not surprisingly, this made it difficult to create a reliable business around the art of brewing.

Cultivation and propagation have changed all that.

"In our modern world, we have the capability to not only utilize a wide range of pure yeast strains, but to also control the environment in which the yeasts perform their valuable service," yeast propagation firm Wyeast writes on its web site. "It is important for the modern brewer to not only know and understand the yeast strains available for use but to also understand how manipulating the environment in which the yeasts perform (wort, must, or dough) can drastically alter the finished product (beer, wine, or bread). The endless combinations of ingredients, yeast strains, equipment designs, and brewing techniques are what make brewing a fascinating and sometimes all-consuming hobby."

Geneticist Dr. Nicole Garneau's office is tucked away in the administrative wing of the Denver Museum of Nature and Science, situated in a small corner overlooking Colorado Boulevard. City Park, Denver's largest downtown green space, effectively surrounds the museum on three sides, forming a 330-acre boundary between the 500,000-square-foot facility—the Rocky Mountain region's oldest science- and education-focused municipal institution, founded in 1900—and the city itself. Tasked with igniting the community's "passion for nature and science," the museum hosts a wide range of exhibits and supports research in fields ranging from zoology, to geology, to paleontology and planetary science, enabling the scientists involved to both make new discoveries and share them with the general public.

But that's not why I ended up in Dr. Garneau's office one Wednesday afternoon in May 2015, braving the near-endless crowds of school kids and tourists in the parking lot.

I was there to talk about beer.

Turns out, in addition to her work as a research geneticist and health sciences expert, Garneau is something of a well-known beer enthusiast. She drinks it, she researches it, and she loves to talk about it. Being a scientist, of course, when she gets down into the details of brewed beverages, though, she can really get into the weeds of flavor profiles, chemical compounds, and metabolic pathways, bringing new clarity to the science of brewing and why certain flavors express themselves in beer as they do. When I visited, for instance, she was in the midst of a months-long project with Lindsay Guerdrum, who works full time as a sensory analyst at New Belgium Brewing, to develop a new flavor wheel, or set of flavor standards, for beer. Unlike wine, for which flavors were well defined (nutty, caramel, berry, spicy, citrus, etc.) by the Wine Aroma Wheel developed by University of California at Davis professor emeritus Ann C. Noble in the 1980s, similar standards for beer were, at the time of my visit with Garneau, woefully out of date. "This work is really about trying to make the behind-the-scenes work on flavor scientifically sound, which it hasn't been for a really long time," she told me. "There was a really good start at it, then it never got picked back up. A lot of the original work, like the flavor wheel, hasn't been updated in almost forty years, and it's all based on lagers and pils. It blows my mind that none of this work has been updated."

And that's just part of her involvement with the craft beer community. In the summer of 2013, she launched a joint project with the Denver Beer Company, local craft brewer, in which Garneau and her research staff gathered wild yeast from outside the museum's door in City Park and the brewers made a beer with it.

"The backstory is that we have a good partnership with Denver Beer Company, and they're always willing to experiment and do weird stuff with us," she says. "Every year, we host an event called Science on Tap. Essentially, it boils down to brewing a special beer that's an experiment with them, me getting up on the bar after that beer is brewed, and talking super 'beer nerdy' about one of the aspects of the beer."

The goal that year, she says, was to focus the program on yeast to better identify and highlight the role that different strains and applications have on beer flavors. Yeast was something that had always interested Patrick Crawford and Charlie Berger, the cofounders and owners of the Denver Beer Company, so they, as she remembers it, more or less showed up at Garneau's lab a few weeks before the program and announced that they wanted to explore yeast by brewing up a batch of "wild" beer.

"We were like, 'all right, let's try it,'" she remembers. "Go out, swab, collect whatever you're going to collect and isolate yeast from that. Once you've isolated the yeast, though, you have to figure out, 'is it even a fermenting yeast?' Only a small percentage of yeast are. Then, at that point, if it is a fermenting yeast, can we isolate enough of it to make beer?"

And that's not exactly easy. Of the roughly 1,600 different yeast species available in the wild, less than 5 percent are capable of fermentation. The rest simply occupy a solution, convert the sugars in it into energy, and don't give off alcohol as a by-product. Truth is, the odds of this type of experiment actually working out and creating a good beer aren't great, but by collecting wild yeast in bulk it is theoretically possible to isolate a fermenting strain.

For both Garneau and the brewers at Denver Beer Company, the wild yeast project was really about breaking new ground rather than making an award-winning beer. Not only were they unsure they would be able to collect enough of the right kind of yeast to make beer, they weren't even sure they would have enough time to complete the fermentation process with it if they tried. Ultimately, and with some help with the yeast professionals at White Labs telling them what to shoot for in their yeast collection and isolation, they made a go of it, even getting a beer brewed in time for their event. In the end, though, they did not end up with a fermenting yeast, so what they served their guests at Denver Beer Company was essentially more of a dressed-up wort than a true, fermented beer. But the reviews were good nonetheless.

"It was really funny," Garneau says, "because we let people taste it before we talked about it. People were like, 'Oh I love this.' And we were just like, 'It's sugar, of course you love it.' There was nothing in there; it was just sugar with cool, good beer flavoring. The hops and everything were in it, but there was no alcohol in it. Obviously, if we did partner on a yeast experiment again,

we'd have to do it far enough in advance that I could actually order plates that had yeast broth, not just the broth we had available upstairs in the lab, and we would make sure we had the right nutrients. And I would, at the end of the day, get stuff sequenced so we knew what we were working with. It was just a funny situation. We tried it; it was fun."

The fact that yeast remains such a little-understood part of the brewing process strikes Garneau as borderline unfair. In this day and age, with all of the focus being placed on what we are eating and drinking, including where it comes from and how it's prepared, it's clear that people really want to better understand their food. And although, yes, chemistry can be complicated, it doesn't take much chemical knowledge to understand what yeast is and what it's doing during the fermentation process.

All it does, she says, is metabolize the sugars in the wort (in the case of beer) to create energy: it's eating.

"The end product, the main product, is going to be the same," she says. "You've got CO_2. The whole point of it is energy, right? Yeast doesn't give a rat's 'you know what' about the CO_2 by-product or the alcohol. The point is to get energy out of it. In this case, of course, the fermentation product is alcohol. But there's these side channels where if you have a molecule that doesn't fully go through a process, it can kind of kick out to a minor pathway and have some sort of reaction where it becomes something else. It kind of gets diverted inadvertently, but the main product, no matter what yeast you're talking about, your main pathway is the same."

It's these minor pathways that can really make a difference in terms of the flavor and character of a final beer, because they're the part of the process (to use Garneau's words) that "kicks out" different chemicals and esters as they convert the sugars in the raw beer to alcohol. The result of these metabolic changes vary based on the type of yeast and the different ingredients used in the wort, and they can result in vast flavor differences in beer because they aren't just dependent on the yeast itself but also the environment the yeast is living in.

"It's just like with humans, right?" Garneau says. "Your genetics doesn't tell me exactly who you are; it's about nature and nurture. It's the same thing with yeast. There are ways you can manipulate the environment to get more of those side products if you want more of that, depending on whatever the flavor profile is that you're shooting for, or whatever style you're shooting for. Big picture, the major pathway is the same, no matter what end product you're talking about, however, what makes it so interesting are all these minor metabolic pathways that come out depending on the yeast strain, and they have a big impact on flavor."

The next step for brewers in all this will likely be custom yeast strains manipulated and cultivated just for their specific recipes. This had yet to take off at any real scale as of 2015, but many of the yeast propagation companies were already working on yeast-specific products for clients, and the industry had begun to show some interest in these new options. What's more, as craft breweries grow and begin to have more investable capital to support work like this, Garneau hopes they will be able to lay the foundation for new academic research into brewing science at the institutional level.

"The idea is, if we really want this, if we're becoming a very sophisticated industry and we want to have people recognize and understand where beer can go in terms of flavor, you got to put your money where your mouth is," she says. "People have to start investing in the research and those research dollars are probably not going to come from the traditional places [because of limitations on grant funding for the study of alcoholic beverages]."

Why do we need to talk about flavor in beer, or to describe the various chemical processes going on in the background? Because it will promote a deeper understanding of the category and encourage the creation of better, more interesting beers. It's like the revolution the wine industry went through in the 1970s and '80s, when the now-standardized language of wine came into widespread use. This allowed everyday people, as well as industry professionals,

to describe and talk about the flavors in a given wine in a set, understood way that made sense to everyone. This development, which really began in earnest with the UC Davis Wine Aroma Wheel project, not only made it easier for winemakers to sell their wines—describing the oak character or tannin level of their products more accurately so that potential buyers could understand what they were getting before even opening the bottle—but for drinkers to better understand what was going on in the glass. For the first time, it became possible to pick up a bottle of wine from an unknown producer and, simply by reading the winemaker's description of it, have a generally good idea what it was going to taste like. That fact encouraged experimentation in both winemaking and buying, leveling the playing field between the establishment producers at the time (which were mostly European legacy brands) and upstarts in the United States, Australia, and elsewhere. Buying wine went from a process of identifying a particular producer or chateau to a more straightforward discussion of flavor: "This wine is good, it tastes of fruit, smoke and white pepper, and it will pair nicely with a steak or other grilled meats."

And this is what Garneau wants for beer, and her ongoing flavor wheel project is the first step in that process.

"The idea of all this is, how can we say we have styles and give directions to brewers, and give direction to people who are the consumers, if we don't have a standardized language for them to use?" she asks. "Standardized language is very important. If you're going to communicate to me, if you're using a certain word, it better mean the same thing to me as it does to you or else we're not communicating properly. We don't have that in beer right now. I think it started off that way when in the seventies we were really working with post-Prohibition beer styles, your typical Germans for the most part, lagers, pilsners, etc. A lot of the preliminary work that was done on building the standardized language so we could communicate about beer was done then and around those styles."

The eventual goal of this is the creation of a new tool that people can use in their daily beer-discussing lives, taking the whole experience of making, buying, and drinking beer to another level of understanding and appreciation. Say a brewer is preparing a recipe he wants to taste a certain way, either because it's based on a certain set of ingredients or is a variation on a common style. With Garneau's tool, he will eventually be able to look at the flavor profile he wants with a full understanding of everything that goes into making it, allowing him to make better decisions at the very start with the end goal in mind. Maybe the flavor he wants for his beer comes from a certain strain of yeast or from aging in a certain kind of wood barrel. That's the next step in the process: getting from ingredients to flavors. If you want your beer to taste like this, you need to know that this part of the flavor profile comes from a certain yeast, this part comes from a particular malt, and this part comes from a certain kind of hops.

A fair amount of peer-reviewed, scientific research goes into the type of database that Garneau is working on. To start with, there are already a number of different "language" databases, or sets of shared knowledge, around the areas of non-beer-related sensory science that will need to be merged together to ensure that everyone is speaking the same way about beer. It's not just about sensory work, either, as there are a number of general flavor databases out there, as well, both in the United States and overseas, that will need to be considered, all dialing down the flavors and characteristics that we understand about beer to their origins.

Do brewers care about these sorts of details? Will it have an impact on the products they make? It depends. After all, much of the day-to-day work of brewing beer involves working from established recipes and within known parameters. When brewers want to tinker with their flavors, they often just do it; they brew small pilot batches and experiment with the variables of their recipes on a small scale. Why that fresh hopped Belgian-style IPA isn't as hoppy as expected may not be a huge concern at the end of the day, as long as the beer is good and it can be sold. Adjustments, if they are even needed, can be made in future batches.

But that could soon be changing, driven in part by motivated, experimental nanobrewers in search of the next big thing in beer. Some of these small brewers are even now putting together tasting panels and doing work in the realm of flavor, isolating both what they know about their beers and what they don't yet know. Even larger brewers—from craft operations like Sierra Nevada to macrobrewers like MillerCoors—are now investing in sensory science, even going so far as to keep PhDs on staff, to make sure that everything they do in the brewhouse is repeatable and consistent from batch to batch and over hundreds of barrels. So much of the industry's bottom line is tied up in reliability like this that they need to fully understand what they have going on in terms of flavor.

Still, Garneau is realistic about the process.

"At this point, I'm sure some brewers are like, 'I don't really care [about the science] as long as you give me that tool and I can use it to make better beer,'" she says.

CHAPTER 9

BUSINESS

"How they start the business is how it will progress, and that could go any number of ways. They all start relatively small, but some want to stay small and some don't. Some go in with the intention of staying small and decide to expand later, while some go in with the intention of expansion as part of the business model. There is no set answer. There is no blanket statement regarding any nanobrewery, much like there is regarding any other craft brewery."

—Matt Simpson, "The Beer Sommelier"

Sam Calagione knows how to write.

In 2011, Calagione, the founder and head brewer of Dogfish Head Craft Brewery, a now national operation based in Rehoboth Beach, Delaware, wrote a book about his twenty-plus years in the beer industry titled, appropriately, *Brewing Up a Business*. In it, he outlines his early entrepreneurial efforts, his business philosophies, his leadership theories, and his approach to work-life balance in this very competitive industry.

The book has, over the last several years, developed a bit of a reputation as one of the better books on commercial craft brewing, a business story that just about everyone in the industry has read and can relate to. It's well written and entertaining, for sure, but that should come as no surprise because, in 1995, when Calagione started the original Dogfish Head Brewing & Eats brewpub, he had just dropped out of the creative writing program at Columbia University in New York, effectively giving up on his lifelong dream of being a writer to start his own beach brewpub. He raised about $180,000 from friends and family to seed the venture and was soon brewing his unique take on beer styles—he used green raisins in his Raison D'Etre, for example, and a blue-green algae called spirulina in the company's Verdi Verdi Good lager to give it an intense but 100-percent natural green color—on a glorified homebrewing system in the kitchen. Today, Dogfish Head produces roughly 175,000 barrels of beer annually, and its products are distributed almost nationwide.

Calagione's insights into the culture of the brewing business, along with his beers, have won him many admirers.

"Entrepreneurs are fueled by risk and an inherent desire to make their mark in their world," he writes in *Brewing Up a Business*. In growing Dogfish Head, I've done a lot of things right and a lot of things wrong. What I am most proud of is having done so many things. Everybody has dreams and ideas; our imaginations should be our most treasured assets. But the self-esteem and courage needed to continually face the Sisyphean task of moving your ideas from imagination toward reality are what propel an entrepreneur forward. Everyone has great ideas, but successful businesspeople tend to be better at *executing* great ideas. The sense of accomplishment that comes with this execution gives us the buzz we seek. The buzz would not be half as resonant if there were no risk involved."

And that points to a universal truth, not just among brewery founders, but among entrepreneurs of all sorts: it's not the idea; it's the execution. It's about showing up every day and working your plan until you've reached your goal. It likely won't be fast and it certainly won't be easy, but in business (particularly small business) there is only one way to go, and that's forward.

"When we opened our doors, we had the dubious distinction of being the smallest brewery in the country," Calagione writes. "Today Dogfish Head is among the fastest-growing breweries in the United States. We are still tiny, but we are growing strong. . . . The one thing we have successfully done is establish a small brand that stands for quality and innovation. We have built this brand through our own belief and determination in what we are doing and the shared belief of our coworkers and customers."

That was the approach that Jesse Brookstein, Jon Cross, and Chris Bell took when they opened Call to Arms Brewing Company on Denver's far north side in 2015. The three had met while working at Avery Brewing Company in Boulder, Colorado, one of the oldest and more-established craft brewing operations in the state, so they brought a fair amount of industry experience and real-world brewing expertise to the table when they decided to break out and start their own place.

That's not to say it was any easier for them to start up than it would have been for your average homebrewer.

"I've always wanted to start my own thing," Brookstein told me over pints at Call to Arms' then-brand-new tasting room, set up in the style of a modern English pub, complete with a canopied wooden bar and exposed beams. The space is located in a former auto shop that had once housed the one-time landlord's collection of vintage motorcycles. "And I've got notes about it from back in 2003 when I was doing a semester abroad. I was hoping to go home to New York and open a bar up there. I've always wanted to open a bar. But if you'd asked me three to four years into my Avery career if I wanted to own my own brewery, I probably would have looked at you like you're crazy because it's so expensive and all that. But once Chris and John and I all started really talking about it, it just kind of came together."

That's a little bit of an exaggeration, of course. In fact, he later admitted that the entire process—from putting together the business plan, to soliciting the investors, to finding and building out the location, to actually developing the recipes and brewing the beer and finally opening the doors—took two years, two months, and six days in total. Not exactly an overnight process. But it points to the many different challenges that go into starting a commercial brewery, even at a somewhat limited scale. Call to Arms, for example, opened with a ten-barrel brewing system, including five ten-barrel fermenters, as well as a three-hundred-gallon open fermenter for sour beers, and plans to eventually start a barrel-aging program. Their beer list is diverse, featuring styles from all over the world, with a lot of unique twists on classic flavors that reflect the founders' diverse experience in the world of beer.

The first step in the process of making the brewery a reality was working out the partnership. Given his longtime dream of owning and operating a bar,

Jesse handles all of the front-of-house concerns, while Jon, the biology major of the group, manages all the brewing and cellar work in the back, everything that goes into producing the actual beer. Bell is the controller, overseeing the financial side of the operation and, by his own admission, pretty much everything else that the other two can't get to. (When I visited, he was going back and forth between the accounting system in the back and the oversized garage doors in the front of the house, trying to come up with a way to keep water from leaking into the slightly-below-grade bar space every time it rains.) The group wrote their business plan with a focus on the Tennyson Street neighborhood where they ended up.

"We looked at Washington Park, we looked at downtown, and we just kept on coming back to this area," Brookstein says. "We love it. It's so close to the city but it also feels like a small town. And when you start looking at the numbers, the millennials here, the median income in the neighborhood, and all of those records, it really helped to show investors that we were not moving into an area that's too low on the economic ladder. It was pretty much down to us probably never having a chance to get a place around Tennyson or settle for a place that didn't have the adequate flooring needed. But then this place popped up—Chris found it before our brokers even did—and in the renderings, they had barrels in the background, so we were thinking, 'Wow, maybe they're looking for a brewery in here.' So we emailed them and then it was pretty much, 'Well, here we go.'"

And then there was the question of money. Having worked in the brewing industry for so long—the three put in more than thirteen years combined at Avery, in addition to other brewery work throughout the years—turned out to be a double-edged sword for the founders. They had the skills they needed to create their own commercial brewery, but years working in low-paying brewing jobs had left them with very little investable capital to get their venture off the ground. "The number one question we got when we started looking at spaces was 'How much skin have you got in the game?' you know?" Brookstein says. Their combined savings, to put it mildly, was simply not enough to fund what became a six-figure venture pretty quickly, from the build-out of the space, to installing the brewhouse, to hiring and training the staff, and more.

So they reached out to potential investors, starting with friends and family before moving on to accredited investors from out of state and other more professional sources. Bell's father works in finance and helped them put together the business plan. "After we wrote this thing that was like seventy-five pages, we were so proud of ourselves," Brookstein says. "And he basically was like, 'All right great, now you're going to edit that down to about ten pages.' So we edit it down and he was like, 'All right, cool. And by the way, no real money investor is actually going to read this so you've got to make a five-page version of it.' It was . . . a process." The experience enabled them not only to make their case but also solidify the plans for the business overall. (And that's not all. They also put together a packet of plans and details as a way to sell themselves to potential landlords, complete with recommendation letters, a sample menu, a list of proposed beers, as well as founder bios and statements on what they planned to do with the space if approved.)

"Most our investors are good friends and family, but we didn't know who the hell was going to invest when we were writing the business plan," Brookstein says. "We just said, 'We know for a fact there's going to be some guys out east who don't know anything about craft beer but they might have a little cash.' I'm not saying that investors don't know what craft beer is really about, but there's this stigma, I guess, with investors where they all have ten-gallon hats and they roll up like, 'C'mon boys, where's my money,' but it's really not like that. They're our partners in this, and they may not know craft beer but they know good business. We just tried to not only pick an area that would appeal to us but would also appeal to them."

The early signs, at least, point to success on the location part of the equation. The Tennyson Street corridor where Call to Arms is located is one of the fastest-developing neighborhoods in Denver, adding new bars, restaurants, and other options on a nearly weekly basis. What had once been a fairly tired and quiet five-block commercial stretch has been revitalized by new residents, new construction, and new neighbors like Call to Arms. Craig Rothgery's De Steeg Brewing, for example, is just up the street, as are several of the area's hotter craft beer bars.

"We feel pretty lucky," he says. "Really everything we expected this neighborhood to be it has been. We've got Joe from Small Batch Liquors and one of his employees coming in here, some folks from Great Divide, too, and we're starting to see some regulars coming in from the neighborhood. Everyone's really accepted us with open arms."

But it's not all fun and games in the red-hot Denver real estate market. As former Avery employees, the Call to Arms founders were all still living out near Boulder, nearly forty miles away, at the time of the build-out and had just started moving to the area when I met with them. That made for some unpleasant commutes, not to mention a lot of trips back and forth at odd hours to keep the brewery staffed and operational. But buying, or even renting, closer to the shop? That was a pretty tough proposition at the time, too, as bidding wars and rapidly escalating prices were the norm in greater Denver by 2015.

"It's expensive, very expensive," Bell says. "I live about a mile north of here in a college housing area, and it's still outrageous. I'm thirty-five years old, and I'm finding Jager bottles in my backyard."

But location matters for more than just the commute, Brookstein explains. "People actually ask, 'Do you live in the area?' People care about that."

It's about community, of course, and that extends to the business model itself. As I discovered at many of the other startup breweries I visited, the brewing community was quickly accepting of their new neighbors at Call to Arms, offering support and simple encouragement as soon as the doors opened.

"A lot of the guys we deal with, it's like they wouldn't even think of us like a competitor," Brookstein says. "Maybe it's because we're in an industry which still is so friendly and cool about camaraderie, but we just don't think like that. Sometimes you start to think it's groupthink like maybe you're just biased and naive, but it really is a great industry. Just this morning we got a call from our friend at Cannonball [Creek Brewing Company]. They're out of a certain hop, wondering if we could get it for them. They needed it, and they've done so much for us that even if we didn't have it, we'd probably go find it somewhere just so we could get it to them."

It's something that extends to the bigger players in the industry as well, including Avery, Oskar Blues, and other national brands. Not only are many of them ready to help startup founders with expertise and advise, but if there's anything that Oskar Blues owner Dale Katechis can do for a startup brewery—from ingredient sourcing, to used brewhouse equipment, to helping find staff—he's made it clear that he and his staff are just a phone call away.

And the proof of this attitude goes on and on. While we were sitting there, one of Call to Arms' new employees came by to say hi, just stopping by the brewery on his day off for a beer. His backstory was pretty interesting, too. Brookstein tells me that he had come by one day looking for work, and that he had experience in construction and had interned at another local brewery. They had hired him on the spot and were still in the process of figuring out his actually duties—"Thanks for giving my fiancé a job," his girlfriend says as they leave. It may seem like a quick or careless hire, but as the Call to Arms founders explain it, many different people gave them each a chance to work at a brewery over the years, and as a result they're keen to give folks coming up in the industry a shot, as well. Bell, for instance, got his start at Long Trail Brewing Company in Bridgewater Corners, Vermont, where he went from forklift operator to senior brewer in just over three years. Brookstein has a similar résumé, starting with an internship at the beautiful and renowned Brewery Ommegang Belgian-style brewery in Cooperstown, New York, before moving onto a job driving a delivery truck for Twisted Pine Brewing Company in Boulder. Without these experiences, both freely admit, they never would have found their way to Avery, where Cross started working out of college himself, or even met their cofounders.

As a result, giving back to the system that gave them each their careers is part of their business model, too.

"This really is different than any other industry," Bell says. "That's what's great about it. It's kind of all of us versus the big guys."

The truth is, starting a commercial brewing business is not easy. It's risky, expensive, hard work, and an intensely competitive space that's getting more competitive almost every day.

According to VinePair.com, a wine, beer and spirits blog, about 3,400 craft breweries ranging from tiny nano operations to the Boston Beer Company were running in the United States as of 2014, up from 1,574 just six years earlier. Craft brewers now sell roughly 21.7 million barrels of beer every year, up 17.6 percent in that time. And this trend has been in place for a while now—the craft brewing industry grew 12 percent by volume and 15 percent by sales in 2010, and another 13 percent by volume and 15 percent by sales in 2011, reaching $8.7 billion in retail value that year.

In short, the marketplace is crowded. Brewing great beer, or even good beer, simply isn't enough anymore. Brewers need to have a unique angle—and for many small, nano-styled neighborhood operators, it boils down to location and community—to have any hope of differentiating themselves and establishing their business.

And that's just one of the headwinds facing fledgling craft beer entrepreneurs.

"Hey, remember the '90s? Remember when the market flooded with new breweries that mostly went beer-belly up?" writes Brian Yaeger, the author of *Red, White, and Brew* on beer industry blog NewSchoolBeer.com.

"I think that is largely attributed to the bad beer they produced because those entrepreneurs only saw profitability over passion for brewing. What we're experiencing today is sort of the opposite: folks with a love of brewing but bupkiss [sic.] for business acumen. Selling clean, purchase-worthy beer falls under biz smarts.

"Basically, oxymoronically, nanobrewers are like professional homebrewers. The cost of launching a nanobrewery fairly resembles that of the beloved food carts that are driving (sorry) the craft of the comfort food industry. And we love us some food trucks. I think if most food cart operators are honest, they'd rather have a brick'n'mortar. Same goes for nanobrewers; it's a terrible business model and if their goal is to quit their day job and make beer for a living, the only way to do that is by brewing 10 (maybe just seven) barrels or more."

That's one of the reasons that the community of small brewers is so tight-knit: because it is so difficult to survive, because the odds of success are so long, and because it's primarily a labor of love for so many founders. But it's not all bad news. The upside for small craft brewers is that startup costs are, compared to a brewpub or other larger operation, reasonably small. For example, a three-barrel commercial brewhouse can be had for an initial investment of less than $100,000, making it a reachable goal for an independent brewer with aspirations of owning their own place. But is it a viable business model? A lot of that depends on the scale at which the brewer is operating. As discussed earlier, it is very difficult for commercial brewers to grow their operations on small, nano-sized systems of less than seven barrels. At that size, they are too tied to their brewhouses—often forced to brew multiple times per week just to keep up with demand at an on-site taproom—to either grow their businesses through distribution or produce enough beer to sell it in kegs or bottles. That creates a natural bottleneck in the small brewing model that effectively limits growth and, in the long run, may eventually force many of these independent operators out of business.

"Brewing is hard work and the margins are pretty slim," writes beer author Jeff Alworth on his industry blog, *Beervana*. "If you don't own your own brewpub, the way to make brewing profitable *seems* to be selling a lot—which is why production breweries try to get bigger systems on line. The cost of a unit of beer drops when a brewery gets bigger and more efficient—which makes the profit margin larger."

It all comes down to the cost of production which, on a nano-sized system, can be very high, argues Dr. Patrick Emerson, an associate professor of economics at Oregon State University whose work frequently touches on craft brewing.

When studied from an academic perspective, he argues, the cost of brewing a batch of beer includes both variable costs and fixed costs. On the variable side, the more beer a brewer makes, the more their variable costs—like ingredients, electricity, and labor—go up. Fixed costs like brewhouse equipment and rent don't change for the most part. As total output raises, then, the total cost of beer falls by reducing the amount these fixed costs contribute to the cost side of the equation, making it cheaper and cheaper to brew a given barrel of beer despite the proportionate increase in variable costs. It's Economics 101.

Aside from the costs of this scaling issue, *Beervana's* Alworth says that the other downsides to small systems are that they can be inconsistent in terms of production and can make quality control challenging. I saw some of this in action over the course of researching this book, as brewers lamented the fact that they, by brewing on a small system, were unable to reliably produce the exact same beer every time like the big guys can. When you're brewing on a fifty-plus barrel system, for example, it's common practice to blend beer from different tanks to maintain consistency from batch to batch and from year to year. That's why the Fat Tire you drink today tastes more or less like the first one you had in 1999. But on a small two- or three-barrel system, each batch is essentially a one-off, entirely dependent on the available ingredients and the intricacies of each recipe. A small brewing operation also limits the number of different beers a brewer can have on tap at any one time, further limiting their reach in a market that has become focused on having multiple styles on offer to appeal to different customer tastes.

"I once aspired to make movies," Alworth writes, "and I recognize this model from that industry: you make a calling-card short and use it to sell financial backers on your idea for a feature. For the DIY brewer with more energy than money, it's a way of getting into the business without taking on a huge amount of risk."

Dr. Emerson agrees:

"So where does that leave nanobrewing? Basically as a foot in the door. If there is intense enough local demand for craft beer and enough beer nuts out there who will go off in search of nanobrews, some local bottle shops and pubs that will serve nanobrews, and a robust enough demand to be able to charge premium prices, then I suppose it can be a way to try and build up some funds to pay for future expansion. . . . But nanobreweries are just a stepping stone—even those who think they will remain small will soon find the tide of economic forces carrying them along. But the good news is that very little has to be ventured so that even if it is lost, not much damage will be done. And the local market for craft beer, already an embarrassment of riches, may get even more interesting."

"So if you're reading this book, even if you're not thinking about putting together a brewery very seriously, call your local energy provider today. Get the process started."

That advice comes from Chris Washenberger, one of three cofounders of Denver-based Cerebral Brewing and a molecular biologist by training (a fact that led to both Cerebral's name and its motto: "A scientific approach to beer. Beer is too vast a medium to be approached thoughtlessly"). Located just a few blocks away from Fiction Beer Company, Cerebral opened for business shortly after I visited in 2015, setting up shop in a part of town packed with bars and restaurants but had very little in the way of brewing activity at the time. The area sees more than a million dollars worth of alcohol sales every month, Washenberger told me, but was underserved by breweries at the time.

Opportunity aside, opening a commercial brewery of their size was a series of headaches, spread out over the course of a year-plus. Cerebral opened on a ten-barrel system with room to expand into a larger production line in the future as funds allowed. They share their site with two other food-service businesses in hopes of becoming a food-and-drink destination for the neighborhood.

"The day you sign the lease, you so should have your form in with the utility company," cofounder Sean Buchan says, "and we didn't know that. Problem is, they're a monopoly so they can pull your chain around as long as they want to. We've been waiting on them now for four or five months and if they don't come soon that could be the preventing factor that's keeps us from opening on time."

And with that, the conversation veers off into the nuts and bolts of opening a small business. "I'm going to call them again today," Buchan says to one of the nearby construction workers, "and the last time [the general contractor] was out here, he said to make sure we tell that we just need a meter. He said the hookup is live. So I'm going to call them and make sure we're on the right track."

Washenberger looks on, shaking his head.

"These are the things that you can't know ahead of time when you get into this, unless you've opened a brewery before. So when we open our second one, we're going to be much better about getting these approvals. I'm going to call them tomorrow and say that, sometime in the next ten years, we're going to open another brewery. Here's my form. Can you please get the power hooked up?"

Frustrating, to be sure, but not a deal breaker for the entrepreneurs, in part because all three cofounders—including Dan McGuire, a Chicago-based business consultant—were all still planning to work their full-time jobs even after Cerebral's grand opening. That's not entirely unusual in the world of startup brewing; easily half the brewers and owners I met with over the course of my research for this book were holding down multiple jobs. But Cerebral is a much larger operation than most nanobreweries, and with their aspirations to add a canning and bottling line, it could very quickly be more than a part-time workforce could handle. Even preopening, the cofounders were starting to think about how they were going to organize their responsibilities between work and family obligations.

"Sean, as head brewer, will probably be full time long before I will," Washenberger says. "But it's just whether or not that will work out for both of us that we're not sure about yet. Because I want to be here full time as soon as I can."

Fortunately, they all had some flexibility in their work arrangements heading into the project. Buchan was a physical therapist, so he was able to eventually switch from a full-time schedule to take on more home health care services and one-off treatments, focusing the bulk of his attention on the brewery. As for McGuire, he was very easily able to manage his work for Cerebral as part of his larger work portfolio. All in all, the "side" work would enable the backers to all pay their mortgages while Cerebral got going, allowing them some more financial flexibility with both the business and their personal balance sheets than brewers who go all-in from the start usually enjoy.

"There are people who can open up on fifty grand, or $100,000, and be very successful at it," Buchan says. "But that's not us. This isn't a boot-strapped operation. The market, I don't think, is going to allow that much longer. Even as we started out, we were thinking about a seven-barrel system to begin with, but we just realized that the market just won't bear it. We had to go bigger if we wanted to survive. We would have gone fifteen if we could afford it."

Even so, the Cerebral founders still came at the business from the "amateur" angle. Despite the investment involved and the scale of their ambitions, each of the cofounders is a true homebrewer at heart, and they planned to bring that approach to brewing and beer—focusing on flavor, ingredients, and experimentation—to their commercial operation, as well.

Washenberger, for instance, has more than fifteen years of experience as part of the Denver beer community: brewing it, drinking it, and knowing people who work with it for a living. He founded the Denver Homebrew Club in 2011 and says that going from beer fan, to homebrewer, to brewery co-owner was a "natural progression" for him. Actually, he admits, it was a dream come true, something he had long aspired to but never really thought was going to come together for him. But when Buchan approached him with the idea of starting Cerebral, the "stars were just kind of right."

"As homebrewers, it wasn't that big of a step from brewing at home to brewing on a full-sized system like this," Washenberger says. "It really isn't. It's a big check is what it is. But there's a lot of complexity in a system like this, and we're just dumber than a sack of hammers so every couple of days we get a new piece of information that helps us build out this process and better understand what we're doing here. I'm sure there are people out there who have started these things and are like, 'Well I'm business savvy and I come from a beer background, so I've got this.' But that's not us. And even on the beer side of it, as far as dealing with equipment vendors and everything, it's a steady stream of decisions to make. Okay, we have the gas set up, now how are two knuckleheads going to lift a thousand-pound tank into place? You know? These are things that we're learning every day. And it's tough, but we're in that zone. I haven't brewed beer in a year; it's almost all purely technical at this point."

Expertise comes at a price, of course, like years spent working for other people while learning the business side of the industry. And even a star-studded résumé full of craft brewing experience and on-the-ground business smarts doesn't guarantee a successful business model down the road, or that a new brewery will even last a year.

It's just a matter of how you come at it, Buchan says, and what you bring to the table. Certainly, brewing industry professionals have some huge advantages on their side when starting their own independent places, including industry contacts, an understanding of market demands, and experience working at successful shops to fall back on. They know what goes into making a brewery a success and are likely well positioned to emulate that behind-the-scenes work at their own breweries. But when you look at the industry, he says, you quickly notice there is no one standard model. You have people who started out homebrewing and you have people who split off from established breweries and done their own thing. The truth is, founders from both sides have done some great things, so there isn't just one path to success. It depends on each individual business owner and their own abilities.

"I think there were a lot of people out there who, when our post went up announcing this place, said, 'Oh great, it's just another brewery that homebrewers are starting.' And it sucks to be lumped into a group like that, when you know that some of the best in the industry started out as homebrewers—Sam Calagione, who's turned down acquisition offers from InBev, was a homebrewer—and you wouldn't say that about them."

The goal for Cerebral, they say, is to be a neighborhood spot that eventually grows into something more. The brewhouse itself is located in what had, up until about 2007, been a series of auto body shops dating back to the 1920s. So it's a huge space, even with a ten-barrel brewing system in it, with plenty of room to expand, adding more fermenters, a canning line, and whatever else the owners need to turn their neighborhood brewery into a true production space.

But what sort of brewery do you want this to be? That's something of a loaded question, Washenberger says.

"We get asked that by a lot of people, but this is a business, you know? And I've talked to a lot of brewers who started small and then they stayed small—'I just want to be a small brewer,' they say. But the level of success in a business like this, in any business, can't be limited at just, 'I want to be a three-barrel brewhouse and that's it.' You know? Because why not aspire to be the next InBev or Dogfish Head or whatever? You want to be as successful as you can and you want to get beer out the door."

So what are the odds that a new commercial craft brewery makes it to its second birthday, let alone becomes a profitable business? Not great, says brewing consultant Mike Mitaro, who has worked with a number of craft brewers over the years as well as large corporate brewers including Labatt, Stroh, and Carlsberg, the fourth-largest brewer in the world. Part of the problem is overcrowding in the marketplace, he says, and that situation today is a lot worse than it was five years ago, two years ago, and even last year. That constant inflow and churn means there's always something new on tap, always something new to try. That's great for customers, and can help give new producers a bump at the start, but can also make it difficult to maintain that momentum over months or years once the "newness" of a new craft brewery wears off.

"Longevity is the hardest thing to build," he says. "You manage to get [your beer] on tap in a bar and no matter how well it sells, you go back a week later and there's another brand on tap. It's very difficult. That's not to say you can't succeed, because anyone can succeed if they have the right product, the right branding, the right energy and enough capital. Some brands take off out of nowhere and nobody saw it coming, and that could happen for anyone. But for the large majority, it's a grind. And I would say that people are a little late in the game at this point, but I probably would have said that two years ago also."

Making the beer is the easy part, but it's selling enough of it to make a living that's hard. And that's a little bit different than it used to be, Mitaro says. Not long ago, it was enough to make good beer—that was a unique enough prospect in the early days before the craft-brewing craze took off—but now success definitely takes more than just a quality product. Everyone has quality products. Now it takes smart marketing, solid distribution, and a business model that sets a new brewer apart from the herd of me-too producers out there to have a fighting chance.

"There are a lot of people, smart people, who say that breweries can be like bakeries, you could have one on every corner," he says, "and there's probably some truth to that. I do think brewpubs probably have a lot of room to grow. But for production breweries, I'm not sure *saturation* is the word I would use, but it's getting awfully crowded out there and there are going to be winners and losers for sure."

Brewing consultant Ed Tringali has even harsher words for the state of the small brewery market.

"It's just silly," he says. "I mean, why do something that you can't really make any money at unless you're really passionate about it, but then just call it a hobby? Why bother going through the licensing and the work trying to make a profit, when it just isn't going to happen? Just be an advanced homebrewer if you're that passionate, but why go to the trouble to license? I don't really get that part."

His concern is that any brewer or brewpub owner working on a system smaller than ten barrels isn't going to be able to make enough beer to turn a profit, unless they're able to essentially cobble together a system from used components and scrap parts to save money. Otherwise, a nanobrewing system will never make enough money to justify the investment. What's more, he believes that to really create a solid, sustainable brewpub, regardless of the market, requires at least a million and a half dollars of startup capital to cover everything from the brewing system to the front-of-house build-out. Anything less than that just won't be able to compete.

"I guess if you don't have to make money at it, that's one thing," he says, "but most people are going to have to make money at this. Then you're basically doing it in your spare time, you're going to your day job and then doing this on the weekends. That's tough to maintain. Most people have other stuff to do on the weekends, so I just don't know how you do it really, why it would make sense."

It all depends on the brewer's outlook and their business goals. A good comparison can be found in the wine and distilling sectors, where small players have flourished for many years as mom-and-pop estate producers. In wine, this model works because wineries need to be built near where their grapes grow, and distillers need to be where they can access storage space for their aged spirits. Just like working on a three-barrel brewing system, those geographic constraints are limiting factors for these businesses, but it hasn't stopped small operators from setting up shop across the country. Rather, the "craft wine" market is flourishing much like craft beer.

For brewers, who don't face the same location limitations that wine and spirit producers do, this likely means that, sustainable business model or not, we will likely see small brewing operations springing up all over the world in the decades to come. They may not have the same lofty aspirations that some of today's craft brewers do, but if operating a three-barrel system can provide them with enough revenue to pay their bills and allow them to share their products with a small but appreciative audience, that might be enough to justify the work in the end.

CHAPTER 10
LOCAL

"At its heart, a genuine food culture is an affinity between people and the land that feeds them. Step one, probably, is to live on the land that feeds them, or at least on the same continent, ideally the same region. Step two is to be able to countenance the ideas of 'food' and 'dirt' in the same sentence, and three is to start poking into one's supply chain to learn where things are coming from."
—Barbara Kingsolver, author, *Animal, Vegetable, Miracle*

*I*f it is true what Wendell Berry says, that "eating is an agricultural act," then the story, too, of what we drink must naturally begin at the most basic, local level.

"Eating ends the annual drama of the food economy that begins with planting and birth," Berry, a farmer and the author of more than thirty books, wrote in *What are People For?*

"Most eaters, however, are no longer aware that this is true. They think of food as an agricultural product, perhaps, but they do not think of themselves as participants in agriculture. They think of themselves as 'consumers.' If they think beyond that, they recognize that they are passive consumers. They buy what they want—or what they have been persuaded to want—within the limits of what they can get. They pay, mostly without protest, what they are charged. And they mostly ignore certain critical questions about the quality and the cost of what they are sold: How fresh is it? How pure or clean is it, how free of dangerous chemicals? How far was it transported, and what did transportation add to the cost? How much did manufacturing or packaging or advertising add to the cost? When the food product has been manufactured or 'processed' or 'precooked,' how has that affected its quality or price or nutritional value?"

The idea of "buying local" has been a mantra in the craft foods space for decades, based almost directly on the work that Berry and others like him were doing as far back as the 1970s. Knowing not only what we're eating and drinking, but where it came from and who made it, have emerged as key touch points in modern society, as many people are paying more attention to the nutritional value and health-related qualities of the foods they eat. Buying locally, often from the farmers and producers directly, makes it easier to judge these characteristics because it removes the middleman from the equation, giving consumers access to fresher, healthier, less processed, and less expensive foods.

For nano and small craft brewers, the connection here is obvious: not only does "drinking local" support jobs in each customer's own community, but buying their beer directly from the producer ensures a closer connection to the source. At least in theory, this should also mean higher quality and a better flavor experience overall. It certainly means more adventurous, more interesting beers than what's generally available from corporate brewers. As Kurowski says, we like to know who we're supporting, what our money is going toward. Buying small not only allows us that kind of connection to the brands we buy, but offers diversity and flexibility that larger, more national producers simply can't compete with.

There are no guarantees, certainly, but the idea is that independent brewers, operating out of small neighborhood taprooms, have a better idea what is going into their beers and how they're going to taste, than a large, faceless corporation. They are also more likely to understand the wants and desires of their customers, taking advantage of nearby resources that include local ingredients, community talents, and even traditional regional beer styles (e.g., steam beers in San Francisco). For consumers, it comes down to a question of trust: trusting the individual small-business owner versus the macrobrewer when it comes to the beers we drink.

And that is at the heart of the "drink local" ideal.

It's not a perfect analogy, though. Although the "local" sales pitch is part of the appeal of small-scale brewing, the idea that buying local always means higher quality is slightly misplaced in this context. Brewing on a small system, one batch at a time, is by its very nature a variable process. Flavors differ from batch to batch, ingredient orders vary over time and, even with a skilled and careful craftsman at the controls, small-batch beer is never going to be 100-percent consistent or predictable. True, that is a large part of the appeal for many craft beer drinkers, and that variability can lead to vastly better-tasting beer. The fact is that corporate breweries, working on large automated brewing lines, can crank out far more consistent products than any nanobrewer could ever hope to, simply due to the scale at which they operate. Note that I did not say better tasting or better quality, just more consistent. At the macro level, systems can be dialed in, blends can be perfected, and ingredients can be sourced in quantities to ensure limited variability from order to order. They may not be the most adventurous brews or the most interesting flavors in the world, but if there's anything positive to say about corporate beer, it's that it is an assembly-line product that is unfailingly consistent.

Still, just as with any small business, drinking local means access to better-tasting beers and support of local jobs. Quality may be subjective and tastes can vary, but the overall appeal of buying local remains fiercely in place for craft brewers, as it does for many small-time food producers due to the wide-ranging impacts it can have on a local economy and the role these producers can have in their community. That's why "local" is such an important part of the nano-brewing story. When shopping at this scale, you're getting better products and are supporting businesspeople in your own backyard at the same time.

In the opening scene of *Colorado Hopped: From Bine to Brew*, a 2015 documentary about the state's locally focused craft beer industry produced by Longmont Public Access Television, thousands of beer fans mill around the show floor at the Great American Beer Festival at the Denver Convention Center, sampling the wares from some 624 breweries from nearly all fifty states. There's upbeat music playing on the loudspeakers and cheerful bartenders pouring sample after sample to the appreciative crowd, many of whom traveled from far and wide to experience the best the American craft brewing industry has to offer. At the show that year, more than 3,100 different beers were on tap, with more than 48,000 gallons poured and enjoyed over the course of the three-day event.

Pretzel necklaces are not an uncommon sight at the Great American, as are full jester and pirate costumes, depending on the time of day. Even lederhosen, that most German of outfits, occasionally make an appearance.

It's a party—public tickets for the event often sell out in about twenty minutes and brewer registrations in less than two hours, making it almost as hard to get into as the Super Bowl—but it's also a working trade show and one of the few times in the year when just about every craft brewer in the industry can be in the same room together.

For the state, though, it's an event thirty-plus years in the making that puts a national and even international spotlight on Colorado as a beer destination for at least one week every year, explains Steve Kurowski, the marketing director for the Colorado Brewers Guild, a nonprofit trade association that represents the interests of the state's craft brewing industry. Craft beer has been an active part of the state's economy for decades, he says—starting in 1979 with the incorporation of Boulder Beer, Colorado's first microbrewery, and continuing with the Boulder-based Brewers Association and everything they do for the industry at large. The fact that the Great American Beer Festival has been held here for as long as it has is just another indication of the role the Rocky Mountain region plays in the global beer picture.

And that role benefits both sides. As of 2013, craft brewers were directly contributing about $826 million in revenue to the state's economy, according to the Colorado Brewers Guild, and supporting more than 5,000 full-time jobs.

But this is about more than just Colorado's craft beer industry. The Great American is also a celebration of American beer culture in general and all of the quirks and curiosities that make it unique.

"What makes craft beer different than a large domestically produced beer is going to be, first of all, the ingredients," Kurowski explains in *Colorado Hopped*. "Real hops and malts, no adjuncts like corn or rice, are used in these beers. These are also all independent businesses, they're family owned; they're not owned by corporate global conglomerates. So you're supporting a community when you support craft beer. The ingredients and the independent nature of craft beer really make it a different beast."

This truly is a local, community story, and that's the overriding theme of *Colorado Hopped*, which focuses on the growth and development of the small-time, "craft" hop production industry in the state through the lens of several farmers who are working on the front lines. While the craft brewing trend has been in place for decades, the support side of the industry—the ingredient suppliers, equipment makers, staffing agencies, etc.—were just getting started as of filming, adding a new wrinkle to the community-first aspect of this business. And it's a side of things that's worth watching going forward. It's often said that it wasn't the miners who struck it rich during the Western US gold rushes of the nineteenth century; it was the retailers who supplied those miners with their picks and shovels. It may well turn out to be the same thing in craft beer. Back-end support may not be the sexiest side of the industry, but the growth potential for local suppliers is significant and can't be ignored.

To learn more about what "local" means for these farmers and the brewers they support, both in Colorado and beyond, I sat down with the film's director and producer, Barbara Hau, in her office at the Longmont Channel, the town's public access television station. Located in what was once the town's Carnegie Library, constructed in 1912, the building has a solid, stoic feeling to it, like walking into a nineteenth-century bank or a historic high school. It's been fully renovated, though, and houses not only the TV station offices but also a live studio space and production support facilities. Hau's tidy, spacious office is located just off the atrium.

"Chuck, who was filming that one with me, his premise when he came to the first meeting was, [local ingredients are just] a fly by night thing, it's a flash in the pan," she says, arranging stacks of DVDs on her desk and fielding phone calls from staffers as we talk. "Craft brewers go up and then it's just going to fade away and they're going to be a fail. But before Prohibition, there were almost five thousand local breweries in this country. There's thirty-five hundred now, in the whole United States. There's huge potential for this to grow. And part way through the filming, after our third or fourth time at Ella J, Chuck turned to me and said, 'This is really different than a crop where you just take your machine and seed it and you hope for rain or center pivot irrigation, and then you just bring your combine and harvest it. It is so hands-on.'"

It's not easy work. In fact, over the course of her research for the film, she discovered that hop growing in Colorado had only been revived in the early 2000s as part of a specialty crop program sponsored by Colorado State University. The early participants in that experiment planted about thirty to thirty-five different strains of the plant on Colorado's Western Slope to see if hops would grow in this climate at all. Several did well, in part because the dry but sunny Colorado climate is well suited to hop production, leading a few intrepid farmers to give them a shot on the Front Range. Ron Yovich, whom we met in chapter 7, started his Ella J Farms outside of Longmont after these experiments proved successful, making him something of a hop pioneer for the region.

But can a specialty crop like hops really be successful, even profitable, on a small scale? Hau's take is mixed. One of the limiting factors, she found, is the lack of processing infrastructure and other support services in the region. At the time, there was no pelletizer for hops in the state to process the dried hops. There are only a handful of pelletizers in the region to process the dried hops, forcing many hop farmers to drive their crops to Washington or Wisconsin to have them processed. Pelletized hops are more shelf stable and are generally easier for brewers to store and work with than raw or dried hop flowers.

And then there's the question of income. Is there really money in hops? It's just like farming fruits and vegetables, Hau says. The first three to five years' worth of work are cash flow negative—going to the poles, plants, training, maturity, and everything else required on a modern farm. From then on, farmers can expect to make a profit on their efforts, but the climb to get to that point is significant. And, given the sheer scale of the competition in places like the Pacific Northwest, which have been producing hops at scale for generations and have perfected the art along the way, the challenge is very real for small, regional hop farmers and those supporting them.

"The conclusion I got to at the end of the video is, I don't know whether the hop industry is ever going to be like Oregon or Washington and able to supply the larger breweries, like New Belgium or Odell's," Hau says. "But I think it will; they have a chance. Sam [Eubanks, with Haystack Hops] says that the key is to have a relationship with one brewery. These plants are only in season for four weeks, maybe five weeks, out of the year. And if you can get them fresh, there's nothing like it. It's like peaches. They can can them, they can dry them, they can do whatever they want to with those Western Slope peaches, but it's never going to be the same as the fresh ones. So they're really pushing the fresh hopped aspect of the local hops, which is only a September-ish time of year thing. I think that's their big opportunity."

Still, while the outlook for local ingredient producers may still be hazy, at least in Colorado, the local aspect remains a strong part of the identity of many in the craft brewing industry, both at the nano scale and larger.

"One thing that's really kicking on the craft beer renaissance that we see in our country right now, and even internationally, is just that need to know who's behind what you're supporting," Kurowski says in Hau's film. "We like to know who's making our coffee in the morning, who makes our bagels. We like to know who brews our beer. And it's that connection and that accessibility these breweries offer to the beer lovers that really gives beer lovers a connection to that brewery."

Further promoting the "buy local" concept, in Colorado, independent brewers are at a sales advantage when compared to their counterparts in other states.

This is partly because of the state's unique liquor laws, which limit the sale of alcoholic beverages, for the most part, to local stores rather than opening the market up to national chains. The system—which limits to one the number of locations that a particular store owner can operate in the state where they sell full-strength alcohol products—effectively gives preference to local operators and small businesses that don't need to have multiple locations, keeping national players from cornering the market with their scale and pricing power. What's more, the system also gives local, small-time producers like brewers and distillers an easier path from taproom sales to distribution than they would otherwise face in a state dominated by larger chains.

Think about it. What would be the easier sale for an independent brewer: approaching a local liquor store owner around the corner or dealing with the purchasing department of a national chain based out of state, not to mention their network of regional distributors? For many brewers, it really is as easy as delivering a few cases of their product around town and, just like that, they have retail distribution in place. On the flip side, small brewers in parts of the country where laws tend toward the traditional liquor distribution model are at a disadvantage, as that arrangement does not scale as well to support tiny, one-off breweries that only need to sell a few cases at a time.

Colorado's system of liquor retail laws is challenged every few years by corporate interests looking to expand sales in the state. In 2015, this effort focused on sales through grocery stores, which at the time were limited to selling only low-alcohol, 3.2 percent ABV beers, but wanted to add full-strength craft beers and other more popular options to their offerings statewide. A group of local liquor store owners and craft producers formed an advocacy organization called Keep Colorado Local in response. From their web site:

> "We are a coalition of locally owned and independent businesses focused on preserving Colorado's unique business climate and keeping out-of-state corporations from watering down our culture and shipping profits out of our communities. We're opposed to changes in Colorado's liquor laws that would undermine safety and give chain stores

an advantage over local, independent businesses. We want to continue the unique success that micro-breweries, local wineries, craft distilleries, and locally owned liquor stores have had here in Colorado. We want to encourage a vibrant and flourishing small-business climate. We want to keep the money you spend at local businesses here in our communities—not send it to some out-of-state corporation. We want to keep Colorado cool, crafty, and independent."

Chris Caldwell, the owner of Pug Ryan's Brewing Company in Dillon, Colorado, echoes this sentiment from the side of the craft brewers, saying in a testimonial for the group: "When I go to Pug Ryan's, I'm not just walking into work, I'm going to see my friends, my family. Pug Ryan's has long been a real hub of Dillon's community, and I'm proud to be a part of a business that has such strong local roots. Our brewery's distribution recently achieved a statewide level, and Colorado's liquor laws allow us to distribute our great beer, while also sharing our passion for friendship and community. For us here at Pugs, that's what it means to keep Colorado local."

One of the key figures in this fight is Steve Kurowski with the Colorado Brewers Guild, who was also featured in Barbara Hau's documentary *Colorado Hopped*, mentioned earlier.

"So this is the industry to put some money into if you want to do something cool," Kurowski says. "If you want to double your money, don't go into craft beer. We're still small businesses. Just like a bagel shop or a hair salon or a nail store, this is a small business, period. Just because it's craft beer doesn't mean it's magic. So, the ones that are family owned, are for the neighborhood, are for the long-term, they quit their engineering job because, oh my god they can't stand another day in an office or a cubicle and they want to have their freedom, and that's their long-term play, to have a brewery for the next twenty years to support their family, and do well, and give some people in the neighborhood jobs, I think those are the best."

We're talking over pints while seated at the bar at Epic Brewing Company, a Utah-based microbrewery that opened its twenty-barrel expansion brewhouse in Denver's River North district in 2013. Kurowski—bearded, dark-haired, and wearing a fleece pullover to our afternoon meeting on a blustery early spring day—couldn't be any more "Colorado" if he tried. Another perk of his job? His office is located right upstairs from the taproom.

Local breweries, like nanos, are becoming the new afternoon coffee shops, he says. It's like it was twenty years ago when Starbucks was really starting to take off nationwide; coffee shops became the place where people congregated, where people got together. And now every neighborhood in the country seems to have at least two or three different coffee shop options available. Local breweries are the next logical extension of this.

"You go into those coffee shops at 9 a.m., on any given morning, and they're packed," he says. "And what are people doing there? They're talking, they're having meetings, they're having discussions. Breweries are the same; these are places of congregation. Like us, we're having our afternoon meeting here. Maybe you're meeting your buddies for an afternoon beer, or your girlfriend or your wife for a beer before you go home for dinner. It's an easy way to be a part of your neighborhood and to meet your friends, meet your colleagues."

Kurowski, for one, isn't worried about brewery oversaturation, at least not in the markets he follows. Sure, producers are popping up all over in major cities from coast to coast, but there are many, many small towns and more rural areas that have yet to see a single craft beer operation set up shop. The Eastern Plains region of Colorado, for example, and farming towns like Burlington, Limon, and Lamar have all of the same advantages for brewers that every other part of Colorado does—including a healthy watershed to provide the water, local access to every other ingredient in beer, a favorable regulatory climate, and a deep history of brewing activity—without the heavy competition that's becoming common in the cities.

"I can't wait for the guy that goes and opens a brewery in an old church in one of these old farm towns and starts using winter wheat from the local farmer, or local honey, and brewing beers in style for that neighborhood, or for that town. I think it's going to be a mad hit. No one has done it yet, but it's going to happen."

He's bullish on neighborhood breweries and nanobrewing in general, in part because the startup investment is smaller and the risk is lower, making it easier for new entrants to get involved. Sure, the overall scale and potential for profit is going to be smaller, but for brewers with smaller scale aspirations, there may well still be room for them in the market. The simple fact is that new operators can now get quickly into the game as a neighborhood brewer, making it the ideal choice for aspiring entrepreneurs, he says. It allows them to make a little money, be profitable, and then save up for the next steps, whether it's a larger brewhouse, a canning line, more sales representatives, a new tasting room, or whatever else they need to get to the next level. Regardless of the business plan, the small neighborhood-brewing model allows just about anyone who's interested to get started up quickly, and that's really what matters.

"It's a business that not everyone understands, unless you've been in there," he says. "It's low profit, high volume to be profitable, and it's limited. Some of the smaller guys, they want to have something that's sustainable that they can make a little money at, and they're not necessarily looking to get to the next level. They want a job. They want to go to work every day, sell enough to pay their mortgage or whatever, and call it good. And that's enough for right now; to me, that seems promising. Those are the brewers with the right mentality."

ACKNOWLEDGMENTS

At its heart, this is a book about people and the work they're doing, day in and day out, to carve out a living in a fun, chaotic, but in the end, very competitive industry. I should start out by saying, given the challenges that everyone in craft beer faces from a business perspective, the fact that so many in the industry were willing to give of their time and expertise to show a lowly reporter (me) around their brewhouses speaks volumes. Craft beer has a well-deserved reputation for being a nice, open, and welcoming industry, and I can attest to that firsthand. I mean, their primary product is beer, for God's sake. How antisocial can they be? But the truth is, I was welcomed everywhere I went, was granted incredible access across the board, and will be eternally grateful for everyone who I worked with on this project.

It would be all but impossible for me to thank each and every person who helped contribute to this book, but I'm going to give it a shot because there are literally dozens without whose help this project never would have seen the light of day.

First of all, big thanks go to Matthew Fuerst, the owner of Grandma's House, for being the first neighborhood brewer to get on board with this project, even when I was hoping to spend all my time focusing on his shop. And, when the theme shifted to include others, he was great about that, too. Thanks also to his brother, Ben, front-of-house manager extraordinaire, for not only making me feel welcome at the bar with my notebook, but for taking the time to talk with me between pours. And the same goes for all of the "grandchildren"—the contract brewers who were working in the Grandma's House space as of 2015—I was able to meet with, only a few of whom ended up appearing in this book. That list includes Emily Thomason and Adam Frank with Broken Spine Brewing, Preston Hartman with Two Creeks Brewing, and Marie Fox with Gunbarrel Brewing Company (which was in the process of moving out of Grandma's House and opening its own location in Boulder County at last check). Thanks, everybody, for letting me hang around the brewhouse and watch you work.

Ryan and Christa Kilpatrick with Fiction Brewing were two other early converts to this project, and I can't thank them enough for letting me come and brew with them on a busy Friday night. The experience was eye-opening as my first time stepping into a functioning commercial brewery, and I also have to thank assistant brewer Chris Marchio for being so patient in explaining every step in the process as he went. The process and back-of-house sections of this book never would have happened without that real-world experience. As a bonus, the sauvignon blanc–infused ale that I watched them brew that night—and I helped!—ended up being pretty tasty.

Also for the Community chapter, I have to thank Tristan Chan, the founder of craft beer blog, PorchDrinking.com, for taking the time to talk with me about the fan side of nano and neighborhood brewing. It's easy to focus on brewers and entrepreneurs and suppliers and investors when looking at the craft beer industry in this country, but the fact is none of this would be happening at all without the dedicated support of the millions of beer drinkers out there, buying the products, spreading the word, and trying out new places on a regular basis. They're the market for these beverages and they're far more active—online, in particular—than I ever could have hoped to capture in this book, but Tristan helped shine a light on that segment of the story and for that I'm grateful.

At Baere Brewing Company (pronounced "Bear"), cofounders Ryan Skeels and Kevin Greer were super helpful, taking time out of their insane personal schedules—both were still working their full-time day jobs in addition to running their nanobrewery at the time of our meeting—to share a beer with me. The same goes for Marc Hughes and Keith Kemp, the co-owners of sake brewer Gaijin 24886 ("traditional sakes, American ingredients"), who were still in the very early planning stages of their business when we met at the Denver Bicycle Café. There wasn't even a name for the venture at that point, I don't think, but their insights into the business side of starting up a commercial brewery, sake or otherwise, were invaluable.

The Process chapter would never have happened without the help of Craig Rothgery at De Steeg Brewing, which just so happened to be one of my favorite spots in the city long before this book was even a glimmer of an idea in my agent's inbox. Sitting at the bar there on countless Sundays watching Broncos games while looking at his plastic jug, DIY'd brewing system got me to thinking about the engineering side of craft brewing, particularly at the nano level, and was really what got this project started in the first place. The plastic buckets are gone now, replaced by a larger stainless steel system—still DIY, though—but the process at De Steeg remains the same, and provided great insights into what it truly looks like to operate on a one-barrel system at the commercial level. The same goes for Josh Van Riper at Odyssey Beerwerks out in Arvada. What an amazing, well-engineered brewhouse, with an open, airy taproom and an enterprise-level canning system to boot. And Kevin DeLange, the cofounder of Dry Dock Brewing Company, and Emily Hutto, his PR manager and fellow beer book author (now with Breckenridge-Wynkoop).

I talked to many different people about the hardware involved in brewing and I need to thank them all for not only taking the time, but also for fielding my amateur-hour questions with smiles and straight answers. Shane Surber with Las Vegas Stainless & Copper Works and Tim Moore with Colorado Brewing Systems, both of you were immensely helpful, and I can't thank either of you enough for all your help. What's more, the willingness to share that I experienced when talking dollars and cents for brewing systems was a huge boon to the book overall, allowing me to go into actual details about what this equipment really costs at this scale.

And then there were the ingredient suppliers. To the malting professionals at Grouse Malting Company in Wellington, thanks so much for showing me around your grain elevator, and specifically to company founder Twila Henley for making the trip into town while under the weather. It was great to be able to see the malting process up-close and personal, and also learn a bit more about the science behind it all. The same goes for Steve Clark and Chris Schooley at Troubadour Maltings. Thanks again, guys.

I searched high and low for a suitable hop farm to profile in this book and, as luck would have it, I stumbled across the perfect spot at Ron and Michelle Yovich's Ella J Farms near Longmont. Not only is the farm itself a great example of a functioning, local hop producer on the Front Range, but Ron was immensely patient and helpful in answering all my questions about hops and the processing side of the equation. I should also give a shout out to Rob Yovich and Morie Block, who happened to be out working the field the day of my visit and were beyond welcoming to a complete stranger, answering all of my crazy questions. Thanks again to everyone there.

For homebrewers, and the authors who write about them, yeast can be a difficult and confusing subject. It's one of those things that is confusing enough to understand, let alone write about and explain. Fortunately, I had the help of Matthew Peetz and John Giarratano, professional yeast propagators and the cofounders of Inland Island. Thanks guys, not only for the explanation (with visual aids), but also the amazing beers brewed with different yeast strains. That really brought the whole concept of yeast as a flavor agent to life, and I know my father-in-law dug it, as well.

The same goes for Dr. Nicole Garneau at the Denver Museum of Nature and Science. Thanks so much not only for explaining the Science on Tap series—and the pitfalls of trying to collect wild, brewable yeast on a weeks-long timeline—but also for diving deep into the science behind flavor and why it all matters to beer. The fact that our conversation turned into the better part of an entire chapter in this book should indicate how fascinating I found it; I hope it adds to the world's vocabulary toward the relationship between flavor and beer, and how categorization can contribute to deeper understanding and appreciation.

As a business book, I spent a lot of time thinking about the Business chapter and the brewers I wanted to profile in it. Jesse Brookstein, Jon Cross, and Chris Bell at Call to Arms Brewing Company made it easy for me, not only opening a cool new place while I was working on this book, but taking the time to—within days of their grand opening, mind you—walk me through the startup process, including everything from business planning, to fundraising, to hiring and brewing. Honestly guys, the open door was much appreciated. The same goes for Chris Washenberger, Sean Buchan, and Dan McGuire with Cerebral Brewing who, despite being a few months behind Call to Arms on the opening calendar, were also super helpful in explaining the work that goes on behind every brewery opening. Thanks so much for the hard-hat tour, guys, and for putting up with my pestering emails.

(I should also take a second here to thank my buddy Dart Winkler, Denver-area brewery attorney, for helping set me up with a number of these interviews. Your help was invaluable, and if I can ever return the favor, you know whom you need to call. His name is Matt Touchard.)

Craft brewing is one of those industries heavy with consultants, folks who have been there and done that and are now helping others along the same path. Not surprisingly, I reached out to just about every nanobrewing consultant in the business and spoke with the vast majority of them for this book. Every single contact was valuable and contributed to the final product, but special thanks go to Keith Lemcke and Gary Grande with the Siebel Institute; Mike Matori with Matori Consulting; Rich Higgins; Matt Simpson, a.k.a. The Beer Sommelier; and Ed Tringali, who was even able to find a phone on his remote island off the coast of Maine to make our call. Big thanks all around for the business insights and opinions on the future of nano and neighborhood brewing in general.

I first heard about Barbara Hau's documentary on Colorado hop farmers, *Colorado Hopped: Bine to Brew*, via Lefthand Brewing Company, which hosted a screening at its Longmont tasting room in early 2015. From there, I knew I had to both see it and meet her, and I accomplished both in a whirlwind trip to her office at Longmont public television (a.k.a. The Longmont Channel) in May of that year. Thanks so much for not only the time and the discussion about "local" as a selling point for brewers, but also for the copy of your work. It was invaluable and helped point me to more than a few other experts in the region, many of whom you'll probably recognize in this book, as well.

And my very first interview for this book: Steve Kurowski from the Colorado Brewers Guild. I'll bet you thought this project was never going to see the light of day, but thanks very much for your insights into the business as well as all of the introductions around the industry. It never would have worked without you.

And, as has become my tradition with these projects, I have to thank my former colleagues from my journalism days—Aaron Task, Chris Nichols, Rebecca Stropoli, Lisa Scherzer, Siemond Chan, Elizabeth Trotta, Kensey Lamb, Ross Tucker, Caroline Kim, Michael Hopkins, Matt Colella, Paul Maxwell, Bill Coffin, Phil Gusman, Nelson Wang, Stephen Wellman, Shawn Moynihan, Molly Miller, Patricia Harman, Nichole Morford, Jayleen Heft, Rosalie Donlon, Caterina Pontoriero, Melissa Hillebrand, Jeff Patterson, and so many more. You guys weren't part of this project but made me feel welcome in your industry and convinced me that long-form writing was something I could actually pull off. Honestly, I can't thank you all enough. Maybe someday you'll see this mention in Google Books. Ditto to Harold Putnam, who not only helped make all of this happen (literally and figuratively), but sold me on the idea that books and writing were worth doing in the first place.

Finally, I need to thank my editors, Nicole Frail and Leah Zarra, along with everyone at Skyhorse Publishing, for believing in this idea and helping greatly to shape the final product. And no book would be complete without a hat tip to my agent, Andy Ross, for all of his hard work not only getting this book published but for all of his guidance over the years with all my other harebrained ideas.

This book is for Kristin.

BIBLIOGRAPHY

Acitelli, Tom. *The Audacity of Hops: The History of America's Craft Beer Revolution.* Chicago: Chicago Review Press, 2013.

Allyn, Matt. "Dogfish Head's Sam Calagione Squares Off Against Budweiser." *Men's Journal,* February 18, 2015. http://www.mensjournal.com /food-drink/drinks/dogfish-head-s-sam-calagione-squares-off-against-budweiser-20150218.

Alworth, Jeff. "Is Nanobrewing a Viable Model?" *Beervana,* September 3, 2010. http://beervana.blogspot.com/2010/09/is-nano-brewing-viable-model. html.

Atkinson, Robert. "Why the 2000s Were a Lost Decade for American Manufacturing." *IndustryWeek,* March 14, 2013. http://www.industryweek.com/ global-economy/why-2000s-were-lost-decade-american-manufacturing.

Baetens, Melody. "Michigan Brewers Respond to Budweiser's Craft Beer Jab." *Detroit News,* April 21, 2015. http://www.detroitnews.com/story/ life/2015/04/21/michigan-breweries-respond-budweisers-craft-beer-jab/26144339/.

Beer Institute. "Beer Industry Economic Impact in Colorado" [Report]. Beer Institute and the National Beer Wholesalers Association, 2015. http://www. beerinstitute.org/assets/map-pdfs/Beer_Economic_Impact_CO.pdf.

Beer Institute. "Beer Industry Economic Impact in United States" [Report]. Beer Institute and the National Beer Wholesalers Association, 2015. http:// www.beerinstitute.org/assets/map-pdfs/Beer_Economic_Impact_US.pdf.

Bernstein, Joshua M. *The Complete Beer Course: Boot Camp for Beer Geeks: From Novice to Expert in Twelve Tasting Classes.* New York: Sterling Epicure, 2013.

Berry, Wendell. *What Are People For?* New York: North Point Press, 1990.

Bland, Alastair. "Local Sake: America's Craft Brewers Look East For Inspiration." *National Public Radio,* July 16, 2013. http://www.npr.org/sections/

thesalt/2013/07/16/202638368/local-sake-americas-craft-brewers-look-east-for-inspiration.

Booton, Jennifer. "Etsy's own sellers flustered about IPO." *Bloomberg*, March 6, 2015. http://www.marketwatch.com/story/etsys-own-sellers-unsure-if-theyd-invest----in-etsy-2015-01-14.

Bostwick, William. *The Brewer's Tale: A History of the World According to Beer.* New York: W.W. Norton & Company, 2014.

Brewers Association. "National Beer Sales and Production Data." 2015. https://www. brewersassociation.org/statistics/national-beer-sales-production-data/.

Brewers Association. "Number of Breweries" 2015. https://www.brewersassocia-tion.org/statistics/number-of-breweries/.

Broas, Billy. "The Birth of a Denver Homebrew Club." *Denver Off the Wagon*, March 3, 2011. http://www.denveroffthewagon.com/2011/03/03/the-birth-of-a-denver-homebrew-club/.

Brown, Corie. "Starting Your Own Brewery? Here's Your Legal Primer." *Entre-preneur*, July 7, 2015. http://www.entrepreneur.com/article/246099.

Brown, Corie. *Start Your Own Microbrewery, Distillery, or Cidery.* Entrepreneur Media, Inc. July 2015.

Brown, Douglas. "Steve Kurowski preaches the virtues of Colorado craft beers from his favorite spot—the Wynkoop Brewing Co." *Denver Post*, May 17, 2012. http://www.denverpost.com/ci_20640653/preaching-virtues-colorado-craft-beers.

Brown, Pete. *Hops and Glory: One Man's Search for the Beer That Built the British Empire.* London: Pan Books, June 4, 2010.

Brown, Pete. *Man Walks into a Pub: A Sociable History of Beer.* London: Pan Macmillan, June 1, 2004.

Brown, Pete. *Three Sheets to the Wind: One Man's Quest for the Meaning of Beer.* London: Pan Macmillan, April 28, 2008.

Bustamante, Alexander. "Elevation Beer Co.: A Dream Becomes Reality." *Craft Beer*, July 12, 2013. http://www.craftbeer.com/craft-beer-muses/craft-beer-soaked-dreams-can-come-true.

Calagione, Sam. *Brewing Up a Business: Adventures in Beer from the Founder of Dogfish Head Craft Brewery*. New York: Wiley, 2011.

Calagione, Sam. *Extreme Brewing, A Deluxe Edition with 14 New Homebrew Recipes: An Introduction to Brewing Craft Beer at Home*. New York: Quarry Books, 2012.

Cantwell, Dick. *The Brewers Association's Guide to Starting Your Own Brewery*. Boulder: Brewers Publications, 2013.

Corwin, Emily. "How New Hampshire Is Helping Nanobreweries Revolutionize Craft Beer." *NPR StateImpact*, January 9, 2013. https://stateimpact.npr.org/new-hampshire/2013/01/09/how-new-hampshire-is-helping-nanobreweries-revolutionize-craft-beer/.

Coulter, Lindsey. "Sake Time: One man's quest to bring the Japanese liquor to the Centennial State." *5280*, August 2014. http://www.5280.com/eatanddrink/spirits/magazine/2014/07/sake-time.

Cowan, Jeremy and James Sullivan. *Craft Beer Bar Mitzvah: How It Took 13 Years, Extreme Jewish Brewing, and Circus Sideshow Freaks to Make Shmaltz Brewing an International Success*. Malt Shop Publishing, December 1, 2010.

Crouch, Andy. *Great American Craft Beer: A Guide to the Nation's Finest Beers and Breweries*. Philadelphia, Pennsylvania: Running Press, 2010.

Daniels, Ray. *Designing Great Beers: The Ultimate Guide to Brewing Classic Beer Styles*. Boulder: Brewers Publications, 1998.

Davis, Kathleen. "The 'Etsy Economy' and Changing the Way We Shop." *Entrepreneur*, March 22, 2013. http://www.entrepreneur.com/article/226180.

DeBenedetti, Christian. *The Great American Ale Trail: The Craft Beer Lover's Guide to the Best Watering Holes in the Nation*. Philadelphia, Pennsylvania: Running Press, 2011.

Deeds, Steven. *Brewing Engineering*. CreateSpace, 2013.

Dornbusch, Horst. "Pharaoh Ale: Brewing a Replica of an Ancient Egyptian Beer." *Zymurgy*, November/December 2012. https://www.homebrewersassociation.org/zymurgy/pharaoh-ale-brewing-a-replica-of-an-ancient-egyptian-beer/.

Dornbusch, Horst. *Prost!: The Story of German Beer Paperback*. Boulder: Brewers Publications, March 3, 1998.

Dredge, Mark. *Craft Beer World.* Dog 'N' Bone, 2013.

Eden, Karl. "History of German Brewing." *Zymurgy,* Vol. 16, No. 4, 1993.

Emerson, Patrick. "Beeronomics: Nanobrewing." *Oregon Economics Blog,* September 3, 2010. http://oregonecon.blogspot.com/2010/09/beeronomics-nanobrewing.html.

Evans, Teri. "Boston Beer Co.'s Jim Koch on Self Reliance." *Entrepreneur,* November 29, 2011. http://www.entrepreneur.com/article/220792.

Fallows, James. "Jimmy Carter: Not the King of Beers?" *Atlantic,* August 19, 2010. http://www.theatlantic.com/politics/archive/2010/08/jimmy-carter-not-the-king-of-beers-updated/61599/.

Fallows, James. "Made in America, Again." *Atlantic,* October 2014. http://www.theatlantic.com/magazine/archive/2014/10/made-in-america-again/379343/.

Fermentedly Challenged.com. "Crooked Stave Plans to Move to Denver." November 26, 2011. http://www.fermentedlychallenged.com/2011/11/crooked-stave-plans-to-move-to-denver.html.

Fisher, Dennis. *The Homebrewer's Garden: How to Easily Grow, Prepare, and Use Your Own Hops, Malts, Brewing Herbs.* Storey Publishing, LLC, 1998.

Fix, George. *Principles of Brewing Science: A Study of Serious Brewing Issues.* Boulder: Brewers Publications, 1999.

Flaherty, David. "The 20 Best New Sour Beers in the World," *SeriousEats.com,* March 18, 2014. http://drinks.seriouseats.com/2014/03/best-sour-beers-lost-abbey-side-project-jester-crooked-stave-boon-russian-river-new-belgium-best-beer-reviews.html.

Godard, Thierry. "The Economics of Craft Beer." *SmartAsset,* January 23, 2015. https://smartasset.com/insights/the-economics-of-craft-beer.

Gorski, Eric. "Beer U.: Regis University joins Colorado brewing ed wave." *Denver Post,* April 2, 2014. http://blogs.denverpost.com/beer/2014/04/02/regis-university-launches-regions-first-certificate-applied-craft-brewing/13364/#more-13364.

Gorski, Eric. "Colorado Flexes Muscle in Craft Beer Economic Analysis." *Denver Post*, December 16, 2013. http://blogs.denverpost.com/beer/2013/12/16/colorado-flexes-its-economic-muscle-in-craft-beer-industry-survey/12625/.

Gorski, Eric. "De Steeg Brewing – Denver's Newest Nanobrewery – To Open This Weekend," *Denver Post*, January 28, 2013. http://blogs.denverpost.com/beer/2013/01/28/de-steeg-brewery-open-denver-alley/8123/.

Gorski, Eric. "Number of Colorado Breweries Soars Past 200 After Huge 2013." *Denver Post*, February 12, 2014. http://blogs.denverpost.com/beer/2014/02/12/number-colorado-breweries-soars-past-200-huge-2013/13048/.

Gorski, Eric. "'Why Can't There Be a Brewery on Every Corner?'" *Denver Post*, June 27, 2013. http://blogs.denverpost.com/beer/2013/06/27/why-cant-there-be-a-brewery-on-every-corner/10715/.

Great American Beer Festival 2015 Guidebook. Boulder: Brewers Association, 2015. https://www.greatamericanbeerfestival.com/wp-content/uploads/2015/05/GABF15-Guidebook.pdf.

Gregory, Spencer. "Starting a Nanobrewery." *Startup Informant*. http://www.startupinformant.com/starting-a-nanobrewery/.

Grossman, Ken. *Beyond the Pale: The Story of Sierra Nevada Brewing Co.* New York: Wiley, August 26, 2013.

Hall, John. "Nano-Breweries: Talk of the Craft Beer Nation." *CraftBeer.com*, 2011. http://www.craftbeer.com/craft-beer-muses/nano-breweriesmdash-talk-of-the-craft-beer-nation.

Hausheer, Justine. "Science on Tap: Denver Beer Co. Serves a Brew Made from the Wilds of City Park. Really." *5280*, July 22, 2013. http://www.5280.com/blogs/2013/07/22/science-tap-denver-beer-co-serves-brew-made-wilds-city-park-really.

Hieronymus, Stan. *Brew Like a Monk: Trappist, Abbey, and Strong Belgian Ales and How to Brew Them*. Boulder: Brewers Publications, 2005.

Hieronymus, Stan. *For The Love of Hops: The Practical Guide to Aroma, Bitterness and the Culture of Hops*. Boulder: Brewers Publications, 2012.

Higgins, Tim. "Apple to Convert Failed Arizona Sapphire Plant Into Data Center." *BloombergBusiness*, February 2, 2015. http://www.bloomberg.com/news/

articles/2015-02-02/apple-to-convert-failed-arizona-sapphire-plant-into-data-center.

Hindy, Steve and Tom Potter. *Beer School: Bottling Success at the Brooklyn Brewery*. New York: Wiley, February 9, 2007.

Hindy, Steve. *The Craft Beer Revolution: How a Band of Microbrewers Is Transforming the World's Favorite Drink*. New York: Palgrave MacMillan, 2014.

Hornsey, Ian S. *"A History of Beer and Brewing."* London: Royal Society of Chemistry, 2003.

H.R. 1337, 95th Cong. (1977).

Hutto, Emily. *Colorado's Top Brewers*. Georgian Bay Books, 2013.

Jackson, Michael. *Michael Jackson's Great Beers of Belgium*. Boulder: Brewers Publications, 2008.

Jackson, Michael. *Pocket Guide to Beer*. New York: Running Press (2001 Edition) 1985.

Janson, Lee, PhD. *Brew Chem 101: The Basics of Homebrewing Chemistry*. North Adams, MA: Storey Publishing, January 10, 1996.

Johnson-Greenough, Ezra. "So You Want To Start A Nano Brewery?" *New School*, May 28, 2013. http://www.newschoolbeer.com/2013/05/so-you-want-to-start-a-nano-brewery.html.

Johnson-Greenough, Ezra. "What Is a Nano brewery and Why Should We Care?" *New School*, August 26, 2010. http://www.newschoolbeer.com/2010/08/what-is-a-nano-brewery-and-why-should-we-care.html.

Kamp, David. *The United States of Arugula: The Sun-Dried, Cold-Pressed, Dark-Roasted, Extra Virgin Story of the American Food Revolution*. New York: Broadway Books, 2006.

Keep Colorado Local. 2015. http://keepcolocal.com.

Kerr, Dara. "Apple to Build Made-in-the-USA Manufacturing Plant in Arizona." *CNET*: November 4, 2013. http://www.cnet.com/news/apple-to-build-made-in-the-usa-manufacturing-plant-in-arizona/.

Kingsolver, Barbara. *Animal, Vegetable, Miracle*. New York: HarperCollins, 2007.

Kitsock, Greg. "Beer: More (or Less) About Nanobrewing." *Washington Post*, November 8, 2010. http://voices.washingtonpost.com/all-we-can-eat/beer/beer-more-or-less-about-nanobr.html.

Koch, Greg, Steve Wagner and Randy Clemens. *The Craft of Stone Brewing Co.: Liquid Lore, Epic Recipes, and Unabashed Arrogance*. Berkeley: Ten Speed Press, October 18, 2011.

Krebs, Peter. *Redhook: A Microbrew Success Story*. New York: Four Walls Eight Windows, November 13, 1998.

Leonard, Devin. "Can Craft Beer Survive AB InBev?" *Bloomberg*, June 25, 2015. http://www.bloomberg.com/news/features/2015-06-25/can-craft-beer-survive-ab-inbev-.

Lewis, Sean. *We Make Beer: Inside the Spirit and Artistry of America's Craft Brewers*. New York: St. Martin's Press, 2014.

Logan, Tim. "Coors Light Overtakes Budweiser as No. 2 Beer in U.S." *Los Angeles Times*, January 11, 2012 http://articles.latimes.com/2012/jan/11/business/la-fi-lite-beer-20120111.

Lutz, Ashley. "This Shocking Stat Shows Why Budweiser Is In Huge Trouble." *Business Insider*, November 24, 2014. http://www.businessinsider.com/many-millennials-havent-tried-budweiser-2014-11.

Lutzen, Karl F. *Brew Ware: How to Find, Adapt & Build Homebrewing Equipment*. Storey Publishing, LLC, 2013.

Magee, Tony. *So You Want to Start a Brewery?: The Lagunitas Story*. Chicago: Chicago Review Press, 2014.

Mallett, John. *Malt: A Practical Guide from Field to Brewhouse*. Boulder: Brewers Publications, 2014.

Markowski, Phil. *Farmhouse Ales: Culture and Craftsmanship in the Belgian Tradition*. Boulder: Brewers Publications, 2004.

Meyer, Jeremy. "Bootstrapped Brews: Denver Start-ups to Serve Up Homebrews." *Denver Post*, July 29, 2015. http://blogs.denverpost.com/beer/2015/07/29/bootstrapped-brews-denver-start-ups-to-serve-up-homebrews/15079/.

Miller, Ben. "How Does Denver Rate Among the Country's Best Beer Cities?" *Denver Business Journal*, August 11, 2015. http://www.bizjournals.com/

denver/morning_call/2015/08/how-does-denver-rate-among-the-countrys-best-beer.html.

Monticello Research Collections. *Beer*, 2015. http://www.monticello.org/site/research-and-collections/beer.

Morgan, Jason. "Echo Chamber Consulting Holds Craft Brewery Startup Workshop." *Craft Brewing Business*, August 15, 2014. http://www.craftbrewing business.com/news/echo-chamber-consulting-holds-craft-brewery-startup-workshop/.

Mosher, Randy. *Beer for All Seasons: A Through-the-Year Guide to What to Drink and When to Drink It*. Storey Publishing, LLC, 2015.

Mosher, Randy. *Brewer's Companion*. Alephenalia Publications, 2000.

Mosher, Randy. *Mastering Homebrew: The Complete Guide to Brewing Delicious Beer*. San Francisco: Chronicle Books, 2015.

Mosher, Randy. *Radical Brewing: Recipes, Tales and World-Altering Meditations in a Glass*. Brewers Publications, 2004.

Mosher, Randy. *Tasting Beer: An Insider's Guide to the World's Greatest Drink*. North Adams, Massachusetts: Storey Publishing, LLC, 2009.

Mount Vernon Research Collections. "Beer." 2015. http://www.mountvernon.org/research-collections/digital-encyclopedia/article/beer/.

Murray, Jon and Josie Klemaier. "Colorado's Booming Beer Taprooms Experience Some Growing Pains." *Denver Post*, April 24, 2014. http://www.denverpost.com/news/ci_25625881/colorados-booming-beer-taprooms-experience-some-growing-pains.

Mutkekar, Niranjan. "A Report on the U.S. Craft Beer Industry." 2010. http://www.scribd.com/doc/48852989/Report-on-Craft-Beer-Industry-in-USA.

Nager, Adams and Robert Atkinson. "The Myth of America's Manufacturing Renaissance: The Real State of U.S. Manufacturing." *Information Technology & Innovation Foundation*, January 2015. http://www2.itif.org/2015-myth-american-manufacturing-renaissance.pdf.

Nanninga, Nanne. "Did van Leeuwenhoek Observe Yeast Cells in 1680?" American Society For Microbiology, *Small Things Considered*: April 2010.

Newhouse, Ryan. *Montana Beer: A Guide to Breweries in Big Sky Country.* New York: The History Press, 2013.

Ogle, Maureen. *Ambitious Brew: The Story of American Beer.* Mariner Books, October 8, 2007.

Oliver, Garrett. *The Brewmaster's Table: Discovering the Pleasures of Real Beer with Real Food.* HarperCollins, 2005.

Oliver, Garrett. *The Oxford Companion to Beer.* New York: Oxford University Press, 2011.

Oliver, Sam. "Tim Cook Lauds 'American Manufacturing Expertise' During Visit to Texas Mac Pro Factory." *AppleInsider.com*, June 6, 2014. http://appleinsider.com/articles/14/06/06/tim-cook-lauds-american-manufacturing-expertise-during-visit-to-texas-mac-pro-factory.

Palmer, John J. *How to Brew: Everything You Need to Know to Brew Beer Right the First Time.* Boulder: Brewers Publications, 2006.

Palmer, John J. and Colin Kaminski. *Water: A Comprehensive Guide for Brewers.* Boulder: Brewers Publications, 2012.

Papazian, Charles. *Microbrewed Adventures: A Lupulin Filled Journey to the Heart and Flavor of the World's Great Craft Beers.* William Morrow Paperbacks, November 1, 2005.

Pelzer, Jeremy. "Cheyenne's New Brew Crew." *Casper Star-Tribune*, January 29, 2012. http://trib.com/business/cheyenne-s-new-brew-crew/article_21d5a27f-4e1c-5baa-bb44-616b18c7af87.html.

Peragine, John N. *The Complete Guide to Growing Your Own Hops, Malts, and Brewing Herbs.* Atlantic Publishing Group Inc., 2011.

Perozzi, Christina and Hallie Beaune. *The Naked Pint: An Unadulterated Guide to Craft Beer.* New York: Penguin Group, 2009.

Pollan, Michael. *Omnivore's Dilemma: A Natural History of Four Meals.* New York: The Penguin Press, 2007.

ProBrewer.com. "Nano Brewery Basics." 2014. http://www.probrewer.com/library/nano-breweries/nano-brewery-basics/.

Rabin, Dan. *Colorado Breweries.* Mechanicsburg, Pennsylvania: Stackpole Books, 2014.

Raley, Prof. Linda. "A Concise Timeline of Beer History." http://www.beerhistory.com/library/holdings/raley_timetable.shtml.

Rhoten, Joshua. "New Brewery Set to Open Downtown Next Week." *Wyoming Tribune Eagle*, February 15, 2012. http://www.wyomingnews.com/articles/2012/02/15/news/01top_02-15-12.txt#.VbEe5qbzT8k.

Rodewald, James. *American Spirit: An Exploration of the Craft Distilling Revolution*. New York: Sterling Epicure, 2014.

Rotunno, Tom. "Craft Beer Growth Posts Solid Numbers . . . Again." *CNBC*, July 27, 2015. http://www.cnbc.com/2015/07/27/craft-beer-growth-posts-solid-numbers-again.html.

Rotunno, Tom. "Inside Anheuser-Busch's Craft Beer Deals." *CNBC*, July 26, 2015. http://www.cnbc.com/2015/07/24/inside-anheuser-buschs-craft-beer-deals.html.

Ruffin, Josh. "Nano Breweries: The Art (and Economics) of Brewing at Tiny Scales." *Paste* magazine, April 7, 2015. http://www.pastemagazine.com/articles/2015/04/nano-breweries-the-art-and-economics-of-brewing-at.html.

Russell, Don. *Christmas Beer: The Cheeriest, Tastiest, and Most Unusual Holiday Brews*. Universe, September 23, 2008.

Satran, Joe. "Craft Beer Growth Pushes Number Of Breweries In U.S. Higher Than Ever Before." *Huffington Post*, December 13, 2012. http://www.huffingtonpost.com/2012/12/13/craft-beer breweries_n_2287906.html.

Schultz, Schuyler. *Beer, Food, and Flavor: A Guide to Tasting, Pairing, and the Culture of Craft Beer*. New York: Skyhorse Publishing, 2012.

Sealover, Ed. "Craft Beer Boom May Be Slowing, Study Predicts." *Denver Business Journal*, August 27, 2013. http://www.bizjournals.com/denver/news/2013/08/27/craft-beer-boom-may-be-slowing-study.html.

Sealover, Ed. *Mountain Brew: A Guide to Colorado's Breweries*. The History Press, 2011.

Sexton, Josie. "Fort Collins Craft Brewery to Close Doors." *Coloradoan*, January 20, 2015. http://www.coloradoan.com/story/money/2015/01/20/fort-collins-craft-brewery-close-doors/22073789/.

Shikes, Jonathan. "Call to Arms Brewing Opens With Its Own Twist on Beer Culture." *Westword*, July 20, 2015. http://www.westword.com/restaurants/call-to-arms-brewing-opens-with-its-own-twist-on-beer-culture-6936161.

Shikes, Jonathan. "The DMNS and Denver Beer Co. Conduct a Wild Brewing Experiment with City Park Yeast." *Westword*, June 27, 2013. http://www.westword.com/restaurants/the-dmns-and-denver-beer-co-conduct-a-wild-brewing-experiment-with-city-park-yeast-5769520.

Shikes, Jonathan. "Prost Brewing Opens Today With a Toast to German-Style Beers." *Westword*, August 23, 2012. http://www.westword.com/restaurants/prost-brewing-opens-today-with-a-toast-to-german-style-beers-5768634.

Slosberg, Pete. *Beer for Pete's Sake: The Wicked Adventures of a Brewing Maverick*. Brewers Publications, April 14, 1998.

Smith, Alisa and J.B. Mackinnon, *The 100-Mile Diet: A Year of Local Eating*. Vintage Canada, October 2, 2007.

Smith, Gregg. *Beer in America: The Early Years—1587-1840: Beer's Role in the Settling of America and the Birth of a Nation*. Brewers Publications, September 18, 1998.

Snow Taves, Alyssa. "We'll Drink To That: Roasting And Sourcing For Beer Mirrors The Craft Coffee Movement." *Sprudge*, February 4, 2014. http://sprudge.com/chris-schooley-beer-feature-49528.html.

Sound Brewing Systems, Inc. "The Truth About Small Brewing Systems." May 2015. http://www.soundbrew.com/small.html.

Sparrow, Jeff. *Wild Brews: Beer Beyond the Influence of Brewer's Yeast*. Boulder: Brewers Publications, 2005.

Stack, Martin H. *A Concise History of America's Brewing Industry*. Economic History Association, July 2003. http://eh.net/encyclopedia/a-concise-history-of-americas-brewing-industry/.

Steele, Mitch. *IPA: Brewing Techniques, Recipes and the Evolution of India Pale Ale*. Boulder: Brewers Publications, October 16, 2012.

Swinnen, Johan F.M., ed. *The Economics of Beer*. New York: Oxford University Press, December 17, 2011.

Takada, Aya. "Japan Looks to Sake to Spur Exports." *Bloomberg BusinessWeek*, January 23, 2014. http://www.bloomberg.com/bw/articles/2014-01-23/japans-sake-export-push.

The Hackett Group. "Sourcing Location Guide: United States. 2015." http://www.thehackettgroup.com/research/2015/sourcing-guide/.

Tiku, Nitasha. "The Way I Work: Dogfish Head's Sam Calagione." *Inc.*, July 1, 2009. http://www.inc.com/magazine/20090701/the-way-i-work-dogfish-heads-sam-calagione.html.

Tonsmeire, Michael. *American Sour Beers*. Boulder: Brewers Publications, 2014.

Tremblay, Victor J. and Carol Horton Tremblay. *The US Brewing Industry: Data and Economic Analysis*. The MIT Press, January 23, 2009.

Tucker, Abigail. "The Beer Archaeologist." *Smithsonian* magazine, August 2011. http://www.smithsonianmag.com/history/the-beer-archaeologist-17016372.

Tuttle, Brad. "The Frothy Backlash to Budweiser Ad Mocking Craft Beer." *Money* magazine, February 4, 2015. http://time.com/money/3695498/budweiser-super-bowl-ad-mocking-craft-beer/.

U.S. Bureau of Labor Statistics. "Employment, Hours, and Earnings (CES)." http://www.bls.gov/webapps/legacy/cesbtab1.htm.

U.S. Census Bureau. "Historical Income Tables: Households." http://www.census.gov/hhes/www/income/data/historical/household/.

U.S. Small Business Administration. "Dogfish Head Craft Brewery." 2015. https://www.sba.gov/sba-100/dogfish-head-craft-brewery.

Van Zandycke, PhD, Sylvia. "Yeast: History and Characteristics of Brewer's Yeast." *http://www.probrewer.com/library/yeast/* .

VinePair. "MAP: The State Of American Craft Beer – 2015." 2015. http://vinepair.com/state-of-craft-beer-map-2015/.

Watson, Bart. "Local Lagers Looming." Brewers Association: Insights & Analysis, February 17, 2015. https://www.brewersassociation.org/insights/craft-lager/.

Watson, Bart. "Loving Local Beer." *Brewers Association: Insights & Analysis*, April 2 2015. http://www.brewersassociation.org/insights/local-beer/.

Weaver, Bridgett. "Growing local in Colorado: Coming Soon to a Pint Glass Near You." *Greeley Tribune*, June 3, 2015. http://www.greeleytribune.com/news/16547161-113/growing-local-in-colorado-coming-soon-to-a.

Webb, Tim. *Good Beer Guide Belgium.* CAMRA Books, 2014.

Webb, Tim. *The World Atlas of Beer: The Essential Guide to the Beers of the World.* Sterling Epicure, 2012.

White, Chris. *Yeast: The Practical Guide to Beer Fermentation.* Boulder: Brewers Publications, 2010.

Wial, Howard. "How to Save U.S. Manufacturing Jobs." *CNN*, February 23, 2012. http://money.cnn.com/2012/02/23/news/economy/manufacturing_jobs/.

Williams, Lee. *Beer Lover's Colorado.* Globe Pequot Press, 2012.

Woodske, Dan. *A Brewers Guide to Opening and Operating a Brewpub.* CreateSpace, 2013.

Woodske, Dan. *A Brewer's Guide to Opening a Nano Brewery: Your $10,000 Brewery Consultant for $15, Vol. 1.* CreateSpace, 2012.

Woodske, Dan. *Hop Variety Handbook: Learn More About Hops . . . Create Better Beer.* CreateSpace, 2012.

Woodske, Dan. *Nanobrewery U.S.A.: A Chronicle of America's Nanobrewery Beer Phenomena.* CreateSpace, June 26, 2012.

Yaeger, Brian. "No-no to Nanos." *New School*, March 25, 2013. http://www.newschoolbeer.com/2013/03/no-no-to-nanos.html.

Yaeger, Brian. *Red, White, and Brew: An American Beer Odyssey.* St. Martin's Griffin, September 30, 2008.

Yuengling, 2015 PR Kit. http://www.yuengling.com/userfiles/file/Yuengling_PR_Kit_Revised.pdf.

INTERVIEWS

Bell, Chris, Proprietor & Controller, Call to Arms Brewing Company; Denver, CO; July 2015.

Block, Morie, Ella J Farms; Longmont, CO; May 2015.

Brookstein, Jesse, Proprietor & Taproom Manager, Call to Arms Brewing Company; Denver, CO; July 2015.

Buchan, Sean, co-owner, Cerebral Brewing; Denver, CO; August 2015.

Chan, Tristan, owner, *PorchDrinking.com*; Denver, CO; May 2015.

Clark, Steve, co-owner, Troubadour Maltings; Fort Collins, CO; July 2015.

Costanzo, Vincent, director, Costanzo Brewing; Sydney, Australia; August 2015.

Cross, Jon, Proprietor & Head Brewer, Call to Arms Brewing Company; Denver, CO; July 2015.

DeLange, Kevin, owner, Dry Dock Brewing; Aurora, CO; June 2015.

Frank, Adam, co-owner, Broken Spine Brewing; Denver, CO; January 2015.

Fuerst, Ben, manager, Grandma's House; Denver, CO; November 2014.

Fuerst, Matthew, owner, Grandma's House; Denver, CO; November 2014.

Garneau, Dr. Nicole, curator and department chair, Health Sciences, Denver Museum of Nature & Science; May 2015.

Giarratano, John, co-owner, Inland Island Brewing & Consulting; Denver, CO; April, 2015.

Grande, Gary, senior consultant, Siebel Institute of Technology; Chicago, Illinois; August 2015.

Greer, Kevin, co-owner, Baere Brewing Company; Denver, CO; March 2015.

Hartman, Preston, owner, Two Creeks Brewing; Denver, CO; March 2015.

Hau, Barbara, filmmaker, *Colorado Hopped: Bine to Brew.* Longmont, CO; May 2015.

Henley, Twila, maltstress and CEO, Grouse Malting Company; Wellington, CO; March 2015.

Hill, Chris, co-owner, Odyssey Beerwerks; Arvada, CO; June 2015.

Hughes, Marc, owner and master brewer, Gaijin 24886; Denver, CO; March 2015.

Hutto, Emily, Breckenridge Brewing; Littleton, CO; June 2015.

Kemp, Keith, co-owner and general manager, Gaijin 24886; Denver, CO; March 2015.

Kilpatrick, Christa, co-owner, Fiction Beer Company; Denver, CO; March 2015.

Kilpatrick, Ryan, co-owner, Fiction Beer Company; Denver, CO; March 2015.

Kleier, Dr. Catherine, associate professor, Department of Biology, Regis University; Denver, CO; May 2015.

Kurowski, Steve, Colorado Brewers Guild; Denver, CO; February 2015.

Lemcke, Keith, vice president, Siebel Institute of Technology; Chicago, Illinois; August 2015.

Marchio, Chris, assistant brewer, Fiction Beer Company; Denver, CO; March 2015.

McGuire, Dan, co-owner, Cerebral Brewing; Denver, CO; August 2015.

Mitaro, Mike, owner, Mitaro Consulting; New Canaan, Connecticut; August 2015.

Moore, Tim, owner, Colorado Brewing Systems and Freedom's Edge Brewing Company; Cheyenne, Wyoming; July 2015.

Peetz, Matthew, co-owner, Inland Island Brewing & Consulting; Denver, CO April 2015.

Peters, Allison, academic coordinator, Department of Biology, Regis University; Denver, CO; May 2015.

Rothgery, Craig, owner, De Steeg Brewing; Denver, CO; May 2015.

Schooley, Chris, co-owner, Troubadour Maltings; Fort Collins, CO; July 2015.

Simpson, Matt, owner, The Beer Sommelier; Atlanta, Georgia; August 2015.

Skeels, Ryan, co-owner, Baere Brewing Company; Denver, CO; March 2015.

Soles, Will, special projects manager, Grouse Malting Company; Wellington, CO; April 2015.

Surber, Shane, owner, Las Vegas Stainless & Copper Works; Las Vegas, NC; July 2015.

Thomason, Emily, co-owner, Broken Spine Brewing; Denver, CO; January 2015.

Tringali, Ed, brewmaster / consultant, Bangabrew; Suffolk, New York; August 2015.

Van Riper, Josh, co-owner, Odyssey Beerwerks; Arvada, CO; June 2015.

Washenberger, Chris, co-owner, Cerebral Brewing; Denver, CO; August 2015.

Yovich, Michelle, co-owner, Ella J Farms; Longmont, CO; May 2015.

Yovich, Rob, Ella J Farms; Longmont, CO; May 2015.

Yovich, Ron, co-owner, Ella J Farms; Longmont, CO; May 2015.

INDEX